Dear David

Dealing with My Son's Addiction
One Letter at a Time

Martha Wegner

ISBN 13: 978-1-59298-837-2

Library of Congress Catalog Number: 2015915201

Printed in the United States of America

First Printing: 2015

19 18 17 16 15 5 4 3 2 1

Edited by Alicia Ester.
Cover and interior design by Laura Drew.
Cover photo by Libby Benedict/Photographer's Guild.

Beaver's Pond Press
7108 Ohms Lane
Edina, MN 55439–2129
952-829-8818
www.beaverspondpress.com

To Mike G., and all the good brothers at the
Christ Recovery Center (Union Gospel Mission).

You saved his life.

Since our son's junior year of high school, our family has been dealing with the ups and downs, victories and defeats, and joys and sorrows of his drug addiction. David has been through treatment a number of times, some more successful than others.

The day after his graduation from sober high school, David disappeared; he had started abusing drugs again. My husband and I were forced to make the painful decision to issue an ultimatum. David needed to enter treatment for his addiction, or move out. David moved out.

His first foray into living on his own lasted one week. He then agreed to enter outpatient treatment. But after only a few days, he walked away and was back on the streets. This lasted three weeks. We never knew where he was or how he was surviving.

After this, he entered inpatient treatment. After seven weeks, he again chose to leave. Once again, we had no idea where he was or how he was living. Having an addicted child who is no longer allowed to live at home, is no longer seeking help, and who has essentially "disappeared" is the worst kind of pain imaginable.

I dealt with this pain by writing him letters; since I did not know where he was, I was not able to send him these letters. I posted them instead on a blog. Writing these letters gave me tremendous relief. It was a way to air my concerns and pain, and let others know what was happening with our family.

LOST

Day 1

Dear David,

Last night I got a call from you. Actually, it was your chemical-dependency counselor at the Treatment Center, informing me that you were planning on checking yourself out. After seven weeks of inpatient treatment, you had decided you'd had enough.

I'm thinking this counselor believed I would be able to persuade you to stay. I will give the Center credit; they really tried to keep you there—pulled out all the arguments, called in all the big guns like your mother and your counselor and the therapist. You could not be swayed. So, I said good-bye. And a few hours later the Center called to tell me that you were, in fact, gone.

So now, once again, you are living on the streets, and we don't know where you are. We've been through this before, but even so, it is still so painful.

Do keep in touch.

Love,
Mom

Day 2

Dear David,

Today I went to a pawn shop. I had never been to a pawn shop, and really have no desire to go again in the future. Actually, the store was clean and well lit, and had lots of interesting items. It's just the thought that all the items for sale here came out of some sadness that gets me. I mean, why take your possessions there unless you are financially strapped? Loss of job, bad divorces, poor decisions... all might lead a person to a pawn shop.

You, of course, led me to the pawn shop. On your last stretch of living on the streets this summer (before you started and then left the Center) you pawned your watch. You told me later that they gave you twenty dollars. It was a "G-Shock," which is what boys your age wear. You had saved many months for that watch, and you were never without it. You know I didn't much like it at first, but after a while, it became such a part of you and your "look." So although we learned that you pawned a number of items to support your drug habit (and just to live), the only thing I felt sad about you losing was that watch.

So, there I was at a pawn shop, looking for it. I wanted it back. I was willing to pay to get it back. I wanted you to have that watch back on your wrist; to be your old carefree self, wearing that big black watch, before everything went terribly wrong.

Sadly, it was not there; some other good-looking young man now wears it. I did find another one, not nearly as nice, but a G-Shock just the same, and I bought it. Since you are not here, I'll wear it myself, until you can come home to claim it.

This watch on my wrist was traded in by some other desperate young man, out of what I imagine must have been an incredibly sad situation. And someone else has your beautiful watch, out of your incredibly sad situation. The grief goes around and around.

I'll keep wearing this watch until you come home.

Love,
Mom

Dear David,

In July, the first time you went missing, I told everyone I knew. I needed support. I needed prayers. And I got both. The second time you left the house to live on the streets, I again asked for prayers and support. Now we are on the third round. We have told no one. There is an incredible invisible line one crosses when their child is missing. One day, he is safe at the Center, and the next day he is gone. Gone. And we have no idea where you are. Before the call from the Center, I was happy. Now I am sad. It is as simple as that. And the thought of bringing our loved ones, and your loved ones, from happy to sad with one pronouncement, "David is missing... again," seems too cruel a burden. The sun is shining. The weather is warm. It is the weekend. We are happy. So, Dad and I will let people have their happiness until Monday. Then they will hear the news, and they will cry, and pray, and offer support, and wonder, wonder, wonder where our David could be.

Love,
Mom

Dear David,

I have a great story to tell you. I am sorry you are not here to hear it in person. You have always been such a good audience. You always "get it" and add to my story with a comment or story of your own. OK, so I'll write it.

As you know, we had to give Finn, our beloved cat, to Feline Rescue. In spite of the fact that he and Patch, his fellow feline buddy, had lived in cat harmony at our house for two and a half years, something went terribly wrong recently. In a matter of days, Finn became a constant menace to Patch, instigating fights and eliciting screams of terror. It had gotten to the point where Patch would not even come out from under the bed. So after weeks of constant tension, I had to give Finn up.

Can you imagine the pain and guilt I felt giving our sweethcart away?

Anyway, the good news is I got a call from Feline Rescue yesterday. A family was adopting Finn! I was beside myself with joy and relief. So I typed up a letter telling this family all the things they need to know about Finn, like how he likes to roll around in the bathtub after it is drained, how he likes to lie in the grass in the summer in a harness and leash, and how he even taught himself to pee in the toilet! I wanted them to know and love this kitty as we did.

So, I went to Feline Rescue to drop off the note. The worker said, "Would you like to say hi to Finn?" Knowing this would kill me, I should have said, "No." I said, "Yes." She led me back to the room where the cats were housed. About a dozen cats were wandering around the room. There was our Finny. On top of a high perch. Surveying it all. When I went to him, he rubbed his face in my hands and purred. I picked him up and sat in a chair with him. He snuggled and purred. I cried. And cried. Tears were just pouring down my face. I thought, "OK, I'll take you back! I'll train you to be nice to Patch! No one else can have you! I admit it, I made a terrible mistake!" And as soon as I said that to myself, Finn jumped off my lap and walked away. No remorse, no regret, no looking back. I dried my tears and walked over to pick him up. He stayed in my arms a few minutes, but he never looked at me. Then he jumped down. Walked away. And that was that.

Right now you would be laughing and nodding your head. Because you know Finn. And that was just him. He loved us, but he could just as easily love someone else. You would have known this already. I didn't, and the relief I felt was enormous.

I went home and told Dad this story. His comment: "Well, in the end, he is a cat." Indeed.

I will not compare you to a cat. You miss me. You want to be home. I know it. Even if you walk away and don't look back, I know it.

Love always,
Mom

Day 5

Dear David,

Last night Dad and I got home from a night out, and there was a message from you on our phone. You told us you had a job interview on Monday, and you needed your birth certificate and Social Security card. You ended your request with, "After all, they do belong to me."

I will tell you. Your birth certificate does not belong to you. It belongs to me. I'll never give up proof that I carried you and gave birth to you and loved you for eighteen years.

You cannot have it. It is mine.

Love,
Mom

Day 6

Dear David,

Last night Dad and I went to the Center to pick up the stuff you left behind. Even though your counselor told you that you had to take everything with you if you left, you had wisely ditched the big blue duffel bag somewhere on the Center's grounds. Dad could hardly carry it to the car; it was that heavy. We imagined it must have held all the clothes you had requested over these past seven weeks. Lots of clothes. You were always cold.

When we got home, Dad hauled the bag up the stairs and put it on your bed. It is still there this morning, filled with all your stuff. And I have to do something with it. My first impulse is to punch it. A lot. I'm pretty angry at what your addiction has done to this family. And I am just so tired; I think I might lie down on top of it. I also want to cry, for obvious reasons. But, mostly, I am afraid of it. I circle it like a cat might. What is this big blue thing? What does it hold? Will it have your favorite shoes? Your shirts? An essence of yourself?

It's the essence of you inside the bag that keeps me circling. I cannot open the bag without seeing and remembering when I bought you that jacket, those shoes, those pants. I cannot open it without seeing all your grooming products! My, you take such pride in your handsome self. Where will I put the mousse, the aftershave, the hairspray? I cannot open the bag without smelling you. Your aftershave, your sweat.

Darn, but you have left me in a conundrum. Should I leave the bag there because it is too painful to open? Or is leaving it there too much of a reminder of you?

Of course, you know I'll do what I always do. I'll tell Dad to open it. He will throw out the half-eaten bags of chips (you and I both know there will be many of those). He'll put your young-man handsome clothes in the hamper. He'll pack up the grooming products and stow them under your bathroom sink.

Then I will wash the clothes, fold them, and put them away.

When you are home and sober, you'll need them.

Love,
Mom

Dear David,

Last night, as I was sleeping, I heard you cough. You were sleeping in your bed in your room down the hall, and I heard you cough. And it was such a normal, everyday sound, I didn't even react. Seconds later, I realized that of course it wasn't you. Because you are not in your bed. You are not in your bedroom. You have not been there for a very long time. Still, I did get one moment of remembering the everyday normalcy of you being down the hall.

And the next time I hear you coughing at night in your bed, it will be for real

Love,
Mom

Dear David,

Today I called the police. I suddenly realized that you could be in a hospital or morgue, and because you don't have identification (do you?), we might not know. I thought I should call "Missing Persons," like they do on TV. The young officer on the other end of the line assured me that you were "probably just out doing drugs with friends." Uh-huh. "Don't worry. If something happens, they'll find a way to let you know." I gotta say, about the LAST thing I needed right then was a pat on the head.

I am so far beyond that.

Love,
Mom

Day 9

Dear David,

Remember last winter when we were sitting in the car in a parking lot at some shopping center? I saw a young man carry a backpack over to a snowbank and bury it there. I said to you, "Isn't that weird? Why would he bury a backpack in a snowbank?" You looked at me, rolled your eyes, and said, "Mom, that's a drug drop-off," followed by, "Quit staring and start driving." I was stunned. I then thanked you for exposing me to the "dark underbelly of life." We laughed. It seems your drug use and my naiveté were uneasy partners back then.

Anyway, it got me to thinking about all the things you and your drug use have exposed me to in the last year. For instance, talking to the police on the phone about the possibility that my son was dead. Here's another: having a "friend" (Solomon, the snake) come to my door demanding the sixty dollars back that you stole from him. Of course there is the pawn shop... that was a new experience. Also, I really never thought I would have a police officer actually knock on my door. I had called them a few months earlier to tell them you had taken the car without permission. ("Nothing we can do about that ma'am.")

Finally: our days at the Treatment Center. Now, this was an experience! This place really was quite beautiful, filled with lovely paintings, matching furniture, clean carpet, and surprisingly happy young men and women. Then in came the parents, the ones signed up for the family program. We were a not surprisingly unhappy group, shuffling down the hall in our stunned silence to take our places around the circle. As one of the dads (Dad and I nicknamed him "Hot Head," because he was always so ANGRY) said, "He steals my money, wrecks my car, and now he gets to stay in the f'ing Taj Mahal?"

So... I have seen a drug drop, been visited by police, been "served" (remember that other great "friend" who wanted you to testify in court regarding his stellar character?), received a speeding ticket on your behalf in the mail, talked to the Missing Persons Unit, and walked the halls of a treatment center. I have indeed been exposed to the dark underbelly of life.

I suppose I should thank you. You and your sister have often commented on my naïve ways. Well, this was a sure cure. It's OK. I forgive you. It will probably make me a better person.

Just come home, darn it.

Love you,
Mom

Dear David,

Maybe you know Dad and I attend dreadful "I Am the Parent of an Addicted Child" meetings once or twice a week. To be fair, the meetings themselves are not at all dreadful. They are lifesavers. But truthfully, I'd rather be watching TV, or maybe swimming across a lake in subzero temperatures, or coming across a grizzly bear in the wilderness than having to meet with other parents of addicted children on a weekly basis. But such is my life. Anyway, these meetings are always very helpful. I'm just being crabby.

So, this past Tuesday night, a parent was presenting at the meeting at the Center. She had three, count 'em, three addicted children! And she went through each of their histories in painstaking detail: first, marijuana shows up; then comes the cough medicine; then the heroin. Then treatment. Then relapse. Then treatment. On and on it goes. When it will stop, nobody knows. I try not to look at Dad during these times, but he can feel nervous electricity coming off me, so he gives me a look. The look is somewhere between, "Do *not* run out of here screaming because this woman is talking way too long" and "Do *not* run out of this meeting because this is *not* David's story." But honestly, I cannot bear to hear another ruined-life story. Especially when you are out there doing GOD KNOWS WHAT. So, to get me through these excruciating painful tales, I sing this song in my head that I've been hearing lately on the radio. The singer covers his ears and chants "la la la la" like a little kid when his girlfriend says things he just doesn't want to hear. Not to blame this woman and her stories. It's just that I don't actually need her tragic tales; I've got plenty of my own—past, present, and most certainly future. When I start thinking of where you are, who you are with, and what you must be doing; when I start thinking about you in jail, in a hospital, or dead… well, I just have to cover my ears and say, "La la la la." Because, honestly, it is just too much.

Tonight we've got another meeting. A month ago, the crowd at this meeting was very somber; one of the member's kids had just died of a heroin overdose. Oh, God, here we go again.

Why not give me a call sometime?

Love,
Mom

Day 11

Dear David,

Well, last night Dad and I dragged ourselves to another one of those dreadful "I am the Parent of an Addicted Child" meetings, and nothing awful happened. In fact, one guy, an addict himself, said something that really helped me: "They gotta want it more than you want it." (That is, you, David, have to want your recovery more than we do.) We're a long way from that, aren't we, buddy?

Love,
Mom

Dear David,

Guess what? I'm going out of town today! I do not have time to worry or pine for you this weekend. Of course, the worry and yearning are *always* buzzing around in the background, but I'm going on a road trip. So, away with you, distracting thoughts!

Today, Auntie, your cousin Ellen, *Grandpa Chuck*, and I are going to visit your sister in Sioux Falls. "How in the heck did Grandpa get to be part of this trip?" you may ask. Well, you'll just have to bring your sober self home to find out the story.

Anyway, we are so darn excited! We are going to go on a bike ride, take Ellen to the diner (won't she *love* that diner?), walk the Falls, shop, and show Grandpa where Christine goes to college! Oh, and we are going to a play, which of course is barely worth mentioning, since the thought of sitting still for two hours while people talk is pure torture to you.

You will be missing this trip. And that really feels crummy. Of course we've been down this road before (pardon the unintentional pun).

I'm starting a list of all the events you have missed because of your stupid addiction.

Here it is for now:

- Your cousin Tori's wedding
- Trip to Washington state to visit Grandpa Don on his eightieth birthday
- Trips to Appleton to visit Grandma Jean and Grandpa Chuck
- Badminton games in Auntie's backyard
- The State Fair
- Saying good-bye to Finn
- Playing Hearts on the porch with Auntie and Ellen
- Seeing Christine when she came to St. Paul
- Dad's birthday dinner
- Trip to Black Hills
- Trip to Ely (where you were going to start college)

Mind you, this is only since June! Kinda makes you want to get sober and come home, doesn't it? We'll miss you (again).

Love,
Mom

Day 13

Dear David,

I am taking an online class this semester. This week's assignment: write a "learner memoir." We are to think of a specific event that created "lasting change" in us; that is, "I used to think this, but now after this event, and a lot of reflection, I have come to think this."

Well, I must thank you. Because although I have been presented with a number of "lasting change" events in my life (and wouldn't you know, most of them have involved you), you actually presented me with the *perfect* event yesterday. You came home.

When I opened the front door, that was the first time I had seen you in twelve days.

You walked in, and you looked radiant. I mean that. Radiant. You were dressed in clean(!), fashionable clothes; your hair was perfect (with a perfectly trimmed beard!); then there was that smile. You know, Dad and I have put a lot of money into that smile, but darn, it was so worth it.

I hugged you; you hugged me. We held on to each other for a long time. You told me you loved me and that you were safe. You told me you were staying with friends, that you had gotten a job.

You asked me what I was doing, what class I was taking and why. You gave our dog, Chester, sweet scratches and love; I picked up our cat, Patch, so you could hold him and say hello. I told you that they had missed you.

You asked if you could "grab a few things." We went to the coat closet and you picked out the hats and mittens you wanted. (Does this mean you will still be gone in the winter?) I followed you around like a lost puppy. I don't think the tears ever stopped running down my cheeks.

You asked for another jacket. I told you I thought it might be upstairs in your room. You headed up, me following closely at your heels. As I opened your bedroom closet, I saw you looking around your room. It was really cleaned up. All your books lined up on the shelf, the same bright green walls, the blue carpet, the Boy Scout mementos lined up on the dresser. I saw you. I saw in your face what you were thinking. I said, "You could stay here. You could sleep here. This could be your room again." You said, "Really? How?" I responded, "Just get treatment for your drug addiction. Stop using." You looked straight at me with those beautiful blue eyes, and said, "No." You said it quietly and gently, but you said no.

So, here is what I'll write in my "learner memoir"; what I know now. Addiction is a disease. It is stronger than a yearning for comfort, or a warm bed, or a family. It is stronger than a crying mother, a wagging-tail dog, and a purring cat. It is stronger than love.

This is not a lesson I wished to learn. But, as you used to tell me, "Don't take it personally." I guess I won't. But it is a bitter lesson to take in.

Love,
Mom

Day 14

Dear David,

Have you ever seen me cry so hard? I don't think I've ever wept so hard for so long in my life as the day you were home. I told Dad that night that my eyes still hurt. I cried the whole time I hugged you, the whole time we talked, the whole time we walked around the house gathering up the things you wanted. You took it in stride.

And I'll admit it, I begged. I begged for you to follow our plan for treatment and getting well so that we could be together again as a family. And you,,, well you, said no. Not unkindly. But it was just enough to make me cry again.

You can't live with our rules right now. So you'll live elsewhere. And you want to work instead of going to treatment. And you might have lots of other reasons you don't want to follow our plan, which I just do not understand.

So, I am disappointed. And yes, I cried when you walked out the door. But wait! I am also overjoyed! You are alive, you are well, and you looked great! You are so proud, as you should be, that you have a job.

But darn, I wish you would've stayed.

Love,
Mom

Dear David,

Today, I just could not put on that watch of yours. It is heavy on my little wrist, and frankly, I am sick of it. And I felt OK not putting it on. Because even though I won't see you much and can't contact you, you showed up at my door. You said you wanted me to know that you were all right. And that you loved me. And then you kissed me on the cheek.

Love you very much,

Mom

Day 16

Dear David,

Rumor has it that you have been reading this blog. And you are *not* happy about it (the blog, that is). I did not intend for you to follow this journal; I thought you were lost and gone! But now, thank God, you are found. Dad tells me you feel slighted by the things I say. Trust me, my words are only meant to express my anguish over losing you. You are my precious, precious boy.

So, here it is; here is why I write:

- Because if I don't find a way to let out the pain over losing you, I will surely explode.
- To let others know you've been missing. And perhaps hurting. People love you and want to know how you are and pray for you.
- To express my yearning and love for you.
- To express my deepest fears.

Here is not why I write:

- To blame you.
- To get sympathy.
- To get attention.
- To say mean things about you.

So, if my expressions of fear, or hurt, or sadness have offended you, I am sorry. You are my special boy and I will always love you.

I am here for you on your journey, however you choose to take it.

Love you,
Mom

Day 17

Dear David,

Yesterday I got a letter from a mom saying how much you had helped her son in Boy Scouts. Another mother said in an e-mail, "He's a great kid!" And I replied, as I always do, "I know!" I say it exactly like that, because sometimes I am amazed, really, about what a great kid you are!

Beneath all the pain and the addiction, you are such a great kid.

Love you,
Mom

Day 18

Dear David,

Last week I saw my friend, Julie, in the grocery store. You may remember we used to hang out with Julie and her son, Seth, when you both were young.

Anyway, they have been reading my letters to you. Julie said, "Seth told me, 'If I had received a letter like that from you, Mom, I would have come right home.'" Which is all very sweet, but probably not true.

Because addiction is stronger than any sentiment that a mom's letter can evoke.

You are living proof of that.

Love you,
Mom

Day 19

Dear David,

I can't believe it! I saw you today! You were riding a bike down St. Clair Avenue! I thought, "Now isn't that something; here I am driving down the street, minding my own business, and my boy shows up!" Well, after I got done wondering, "WHY IS HE NOT WEARING A HELMET?" I was overjoyed. Then I thought, "No, maybe that wasn't him." By then, you were long gone. I reasoned, "It couldn't have been him because his bike is in the garage. And I know his headphones 'disappeared' (via the pawn shop) a while ago." After that, I thought, "Who does this kid on the bike think he is, impersonating my son?" I actually thought that! That's what missing a person will do to you: make you just a little bit crazy. Then I thought (me of the overactive mind), "Well, what if it was David? Maybe I better turn around and say hi to him. After all, he is my son." Then, "Well, he doesn't necessarily want to chat with me right now." Finally, "How is it I can't tell if that was David or not?" And that was the cruelest cut of all.

So I kept driving. I think in fact that it was not you. But I'm not sure. If it was, you sure look good. And whether or not it was you or an imposter (!), I was happy to see you.

By the way, if you want to stop by and pick up your bike, it's here. I even got it tuned up for you! It's ready when you are.

Love you always,
Mom

Day 20

Dear David,

Sometimes my old dinosaur of a computer runs so slowly! I'll wait and wait for a site to appear. Then a note pops up: "A script on this page is causing Internet Explorer to run slowly." And I think, "Well, I don't see any script." But apparently it is indeed there, running silently in the background, slowing things down. And that's how my life feels while you are gone. There is always a script of you in the background running and running. Slowing things down.

Love,
Mom

Day 21

Dear David,

I've been busy visiting Grandma and Grandpa in Appleton. As I was leaving their house, I got a call from you, asking if I would like to get together for lunch. Being that I was five hours away from St. Paul, I had to beg off, but promised I could get together any time or any place after I was home. We said good-bye and then the tears started to flow. It's the most immediate response I've ever known. The water just starts running down my cheeks. Sometimes there is a sob with it. You see, I just miss you so darn bad, and you are so sweet on the telephone, and you tell me you love me, and you laugh at my jokes, and you say, "Tell Grandma and Grandpa I said hi," and then you tell me you love me again. Well, who wouldn't dissolve into a puddle of salty tears?

The next day, yesterday, we got together for lunch at Perkins. And the tears stayed pretty much under control, I am proud to say. You were your usual radiant self, darn it. I complimented you on your haircut. "Yeah, I just went to the barber yesterday," you said, and then I wondered how you paid for it. And still I kept the tears in check! Then you ordered chocolate chip pancakes. Really? You were just plain, flat out challenging me not to weep. My little boy digging into syrup-soaked flapjacks.

I had said to Dad the night before, "What are David and I going to talk about?," and he said, "Well, just keep it light," which is not the easiest thing when I am feeling anything *but* light. So, I did as instructed for a while. Kept it light. Then of course I had to get into "Have you gone to AA?" How's that for keeping it light? You said, "No." You said you had no intention of going to AA, that your drug use was in check, and you didn't want to go to some boring meeting. OK, OK. So we got back into *light* conversation. But not before I started asking about friends, and don't you want to live at home?, and every other heavy topic I could drum up. You were so polite. You responded appropriately, and we moved on. You reminded me that this is your life, after all. OK, OK. And after a while, we really were able to converse in a real way. I told you funny stories about Grandma, and the dog, and the cat. At one point the waitress, laying down the check said, "You two are just having too much fun." If she only knew.

Because we were having fun. And we were laughing. But I miss you fiercely. And I worry. And I want you to never use a drug again and I want you to be in recovery. And I want you home.

But, I get it; my radiant boy needs to find his own path. And you are! And I am proud of you. Especially when I look over at you digging into your chocolate chip pancakes.

Love,
Mom

Dear David,

It's been about a month since Grandpa Don died.

A few weeks before his passing, when you were in treatment at the Center, we all went to see him for his eightieth birthday. Even though you weren't able to go, you called him up, and you wished him a happy birthday. Grandpa got off the phone and got a little choked up. He said, "That phone call just made my day." I mean, how easy was that? There we all were, running around, getting a cake and cards and presents, and all you had to do was give him a call? That's how special you are to him.

David, I want you to know that Grandpa was so proud of you. He was proud because you were an Eagle Scout and you were confirmed in the church, and you were a lifeguard, and you graduated from high school. But mostly he was proud to call you his grandson because of the special qualities you have: your kindness, your creativity, your respect for others, your curiosity. Let's be honest, he never truly appreciated your delightful sense of humor; he was a pretty serious guy.

When we saw Grandpa for his birthday party, it was pretty clear that he would not be alive much longer. He did his usual gruff, "Can we have a talk?," motioning me to sit down. I thought to myself, "Now let's suppose I never see this man again, because he dies. What will I wish I had said to him?" Grandpa and I were never very close, and I wanted to be authentic about what I said, not just uttering some platitudes. Do you know what I said? "Thank you for all the things you did for David." And I meant it. Because he took you hiking and fishing and listened to your stories, and helped you build fires, and make slingshots, and take apart old lawn mowers. And I always wanted to thank him for that, for honoring you as a wonderful, creative (very busy) kid. Grandpa answered, "He's my boy." And indeed you were.

Grandpa would be so proud of the young man you have become today. We all are.

Love,
Mom

Dear David,

Well, I guess you know we are going out of town again this weekend. You know this because you will be with us! This is a joyous occurrence in the context of a very sad event, Grandpa Don's funeral in Marion, Iowa. Although Grandpa Don lived in Washington state for many years, he wanted to be buried in Marion, the town where he grew up. So that is where we are headed.

I am so grateful and pleased that you will be with us. First, because for a while, when I didn't know where you were, I assumed you wouldn't be able to come. You were lost, and now you are found. And so we'll pick you up tomorrow morning and make the road trip to Iowa. We'll meet Christine there. The other reason I am so pleased you can come is because I know how much it would mean to Grandpa to have you there. You were a special grandchild to him. All four of his grandchildren were special to him, but he kind of set you apart because you were the *grandson*. The only grandson. And that, as you know, was a big deal. Carrying on the family name and all that. Grandpa was a very traditional guy.

I'm so glad we'll be together as a family again. It would make Grandpa Don very happy.

Love,
Mom

Day 25

Dear David,

Well, that didn't go too well, did it? What started out as a hopeful trip framed by my very positive attitude descended into another one of those "Is this a nightmare from which I will awaken soon?" events. But at least now I can add one more thing to my list of new experiences (such as the time I was exposed to a drug drop, or the time the police came knocking at my door).

You know, of course, what I'm referring to: Grandpa's funeral and its aftermath. The funeral went really well. Very simple graveside ceremony, with nice words spoken by Uncle Bob, and the obituary read by Dad. Then a lovely, bittersweet gun-and-folded-flag ceremony performed by the old VFW guys. It was everything our family could have wished for.

So, how did this day go so awry? How did we drive down to Iowa with you in the backseat and drive back to St. Paul without you?

I tell you, I should know from this journey with addiction that nothing is a surprise, but this stretched all credulity.

This all happened the night of the funeral. Somehow you managed to get Joe to drive five hours down to Iowa and pick you up in your car! Somehow you managed to break the law while driving said car! Somehow you managed to call us at 4:00 a.m. to let us know you were in jail in *WATERLOO, IOWA*, and somehow you were arraigned five hours later, and somehow you managed to summon the courage to ask us to post bail!

We did not.

So, forty-eight hours after taking off on our journey of hope ("This will be a good time!" "A time for togetherness! Healing!"), Dad and I were driving through Waterloo, on the way back home, WITHOUT YOU, looking furtively around for the county jail. We hadn't planned to visit; we just wanted to see what it looked like from the outside.

In the meantime, you actually got someone to post bail, get your car out of the impound lot, and get you back to St. Paul.

Dad and I are once again in a state of shock. You are a clever boy; I can hardly wait for you to find a way to harness all that creativity and resourcefulness into a useful position.

So, do we call this "one step forward, two steps back"? It seems we should. But maybe not. We have not talked to you since you hightailed it out of our hotel room. Maybe you'll put this episode to good use and choose recovery. Maybe you'll chalk it up to one more "life experience." We'll just have to wait and see.

I myself would prefer to live life without these life experiences. Or at least take a break from them. Maybe it's time I get used to them.

Love,
Mom

Dear David,

Well, thank you. I now have ONE MORE new and dreadful experience under my belt: talking to the public defender's office. Because you are going to court, and you will be represented by a public defender. So I thought that I would just call the court to find out how this all works. I mean, are they locking you up? Making you work on the side of the highway with other men in orange?

The receptionist at the Black Hawk County Defender's Office was very rude. I complained to Dad in an e-mail about her. His response: "I guess they don't give a shit about a criminal." Well, I guess when you put it that way…

So because this receptionist was so rude, and I am so pissed off (and you know I do not use that phrase lightly), I am writing this heartless woman. You can pass this letter along to her when you see her in court.

> Dear Rude, Heartless, and Mean Receptionist at the Black Hawk County Public Defender's Office:

Let me start by saying it's clear that you do not have children. Or if you do, they have not yet grown up to become juvenile delinquents. Maybe your kids dodged that bullet and grew up outside the courts. Let me tell you, it was a narrow escape.

Do you actually think I ever imagined that I would be talking to the public defender's office? Do you think I wanted to have a kid going through the criminal courts, in Waterloo, Iowa, no less? Well, I'll tell you. I did not. I do not. I do not wish to talk to you. Or any public defender (bless his or her heart). But I am forced to, because I've got to find out what comes next.

So, a little compassion, and a lot less attitude on your part, would be very helpful.

You were mean and dismissive. And I needed help. So, to get me through this, I have rewritten the script. Your words are represented accurately, painful as they are to read. My words are what I wish I had said, but I didn't. Because I actually thought you were going to be nice to me. Here is the revised conversation:

Me: I'm calling about my son. I'm calling to find out what we should expect at his court appearance. Can you help me?

You: No, we wouldn't have that paperwork yet. I've gotta put you on hold.

(Long pause...)

OK. Like I said, we wouldn't have the paperwork yet.

Me: OK. So when will you have it? Do I have to beg for it?

You: What's his case number? Without his case number, we can't look it up.

Me: I do not have a case number.

You: You need the paperwork. You need a case number.

Me: I do not have the goddamn paperwork. I do not even have my son.

You: Have your son call our office.

Me: That would pretty impossible, you idiot. My son does not even call me.

You: Well, maybe you need a third party.

Me: Gee, I never would have thought of that on my own. Would you be willing to be the third party and talk some sense into my son?

You: Hold on one minute.

Me: Sure, I'll hold a minute. I've been holding for months.

(Long pause...)

You: We can't do anything without the paperwork.

Me: Screw you.

You: (Sigh.)

Me: DO YOU HAVE ANY IDEA HOW IT FEELS TO HAVE YOUR SON GET ARRESTED IN WATERLOO, IOWA, AND ALMOST KILL HIMSELF, AND NEVER COME HOME AND NEVER GET SOBER, AND SCREW EVERYTHING UP? DO YOU? BECAUSE IF YOU DID,

YOU WOULD SHOW SOME COMPASSION HERE, LADY!

You: Any idea what kind of court appearance he has? Most people don't have any idea if they even need to be here.

Me: Yes, most people are as dumb and clueless as I am. I have no idea what kind of court it is or if it's an arraignment or a sentencing or what. THAT'S WHY I'M CALLING YOU!

You: (Sigh.)

Me: Any idea when I can talk to his attorney?

You: No. (Sigh.) Maybe try calling back on Monday. I might have some information. I don't know.

Me: Really, I don't want to waste your precious time on Monday. Especially if I don't have the damn case number, which, trust me, I won't.

You: Anything else?

So, this is how I know you've never had a kid in trouble. Because it feels like shit, and it would be nice if there were a voice in this insane script saying, "This must be really hard. Let me see how I can help you." But, no, you didn't say that. You put me on hold. Twice.

I tell you, lady. You need a new job. Maybe there are openings for prison guards down the hall.

Sincerely,
David's Mother

I hope you can deliver this to this mean woman. It would make me feel a whole lot better.

Love you,
Mom

Day 28

Dear David,

I bet you don't know this. Every night before Dad and I turn off the light, we go through the daily readings from a couple of the "I Am the Parent of an Addict" books. It's quite a sight, the two of us propped up on pillows, reading these little books. Anyway, I read something interesting last night. The passage was talking about the slogan, "Live and let live." What was so striking about the reading was that it encouraged *me* to live. In spite of all the things going on, all the awfulness, all the worry, I've got to live. "Intent on living my own life with joy and active participation, I'll have little time left to worry about another person's struggles and scrapes." Well, let's hope so.

I think that for the most part (barring those sleepless hours between 4:00 and 6:00 a.m., when worst-case-scenarios whirl in my head), I am doing just that. One way I do it is to write. And you know what? I got the nicest compliment yesterday regarding my blog. It came from Tina, "Lady of Dance," my fabulous, awesome, spirit-filled line-dance teacher. She said, "Marty, your letters are so moving. Sometimes they make me laugh, but many times they make me cry." Do you know why I loved that? Because she said I make her laugh! In the midst of all that sorrow, we—I—can still laugh. Because, otherwise, I swear to God, I would sink into a black hole of grief.

As Aunt Liz exclaimed, following what I now call the "Waterloo Episode," "You can't even make this shit up!" And it is true. Sometimes this life is so unbelievable, well, you have to laugh. Not many people could invent these "shenanigans" (this from Aunt Julie) that we have endured.

So, in order to live, I write, and yes, I do try to add humor to most of my writings. I line dance once, maybe twice a week; I celebrate "Free Friday," complete with pizza and *Project Runway* with your cousin, Ellen, every week; I attend every single event at church (OK, so it was a little depressing to be the only one to show up for book club last night); I go out every Saturday night with Dad; I talk to Gloria; I text Grandma. I even secretly watch *The Young and the Restless* (will Phyllis ever wake up from her coma to tell Nick the truth about Sharon?) while I eat lunch. I get on Facebook now so I can see pictures of Christine and friends and family. It ain't much, but it keeps me living.

So forgive me if I live my life while you live yours, and if I laugh once in a while. It doesn't mean I don't miss you and worry about you. It just means I have chosen to live. To "live and let live."

Love you,
Mom

Dear David,

Well, Thursday night added a new whole chapter to the story.

It's hard to write about. I wrote a haiku, an unlikely vehicle, I know. But it seems to have worked for me. I hope that you like it. Or, rather, that some day you will grow to like it.

AFTERMATH

Utility pole
Destroys your car, spares your life
God grants a new day

Thank you, thank you, thank you, God.

Love you,
Mom

Day 30

Dear David,

What a strange night. You may not remember it, since you slept through it. I remember it because I sat through it. All night long in a beeping, buzzing, busy hospital room, sitting in a hard plastic chair. After the car accident, they took you by ambulance to the emergency room. I followed behind like the dutiful mother that I am.

So, there you were, all laid out on the bed, fast asleep, looking pretty darn comfortable. You had been sedated, you lucky boy.

I talked to you, although I do not think you heard me. Do you suppose I murmured sweet words of comfort? Well you suppose wrong. After I got the report that you were just fine, and then heard the news that we would be sitting here indefinitely waiting for GOD KNOWS WHAT, I felt free to say what I needed to say.

What I said was that this situation was profoundly unfair. You got to snooze. I had to sit. Any chance of sleep on my part was completely halted as my relaxing body slid off the plastic chair onto the floor. It was all I could do not to pull you out of that bed, prop you up in that chair, and curl up on the bed myself. After all, who really deserves a good night's sleep? Me, that's who.

And then I had to ask, "Just what am I going to do with you now?"

But you were sleeping soundly, so you didn't have a response for me.

Love,
Mom

Day 31

Dear David,

So, after the car accident, you were home for one day. Then you had to leave. Now you are home again. And I am just so happy! I am singing while I dry my hair. I look in on you sleeping in your bed, just to make sure you are here. I just love having you here. Even though I know it probably won't last.

Last week, the Bible lesson at church was about the Prodigal Son. Do you remember it? I'd like to think those four years of confirmation class taught you something. Well, the man in the story has two sons. One son is dutiful and follows the rules and tills the land. The other son leaves and squanders it all. Then, when times are tough, the "bad son" comes back on his knees, begging to be taken back in. The father is overjoyed! He calls for a celebration! The "good son" says, "Why the celebration? He was disobedient and wasted all that he was given." A quote from the Bible with the father's reply: "...We had to celebrate and rejoice, because this brother of yours was dead and has come to life; he was lost and has been found." And although you might roll your eyes at my comparing you to the Prodigal Son, I can honestly say that I feel the same way! Every time you leave and then come back, I rejoice! Let's kill the fatted calf, or at least put some hamburgers on the grill.

Here's the challenge for me. I have to learn not to despair when you leave. Because you do leave. You tell me it is too painful to be around the house, that you are too ashamed to be around people who love you so much and so unconditionally! I think, "Well, I won't show you or tell you how much I love you, and then you'll hang around." But you're wiser than that. You know, like this dad in the Bible, I love you completely, totally, and without end. And I can't hide it. I don't want to hide it.

So I am learning to accept and maybe understand that being here is tough for you right now. And that you will leave. You are sad when you leave. I cry when you leave. But I rejoice double when you are back!

Someday you will be back, and you will stay. Maybe not in the house. But in our lives. You'll find out how much you are loved by me, Dad, Christine, oh—and God.

I look forward to that day. Until then, I'll take whatever days I can get. You are my precious (prodigal) son.

Love,
Mom

THE
MISSION

Day 33

Dear David,

Well, much to my surprise, you came home again, and you stayed home. You told me that you had nowhere else to go; you had exhausted all your options. Seems there were no more open couches for you to crash on; you could not bear to go back to the Center; and you knew you would not be allowed to live at home. So where were you to go? I, like you, had no idea.

I called my friend, Mike. He and I have known each other since before you were born. Mike is a recovering addict. He was my last hope. Maybe he could tell me what to do.

Mike came over and talked with you. You cried and cried. He listened.

He suggested you go to the Union Gospel Mission, where he is a volunteer, to get sober. I don't know how he persuaded you to go there. When I talked to him afterwards, he said *he* didn't even know how he persuaded you. I guess we can thank God for that.

Because the next thing I knew, you were driving off in Mike's car, headed to the Mission.

You were not too happy about this—you were mighty scared—but, after all was said and done, you realized you were all out of options.

I'm saying my prayers.

Love you,
Mom

Day 36

Dear David,

I wanted to let you know that today I am not worried about you. Because as far as I know, you are safe and sober and happy! At least you were when we saw you two days ago. You are staying at "the Mission," and you tell us you love it there. So we'll go with it! And we'll be thankful for it! And we'll, as my friend Mike says, "trust it."

I told Grandma Jean about your stay at the Mission. I told her I didn't know much of anything about it except that you were happy and sober and surrounded by other recovering men there. She said, "Well, considering all the prayers that have been made on his behalf, we just have to believe this is the right place." And I do.

I just wanted you to know that I believe in you. And where you are. And "one day at a time" has never been truer for me.

Love,
Mom

Day 37

Dear David,

Today Grandma Joan asked, "Why do you suppose he likes it there?," speaking of your latest home, Christ Recovery Center, otherwise known to us all as "the Mission," since it is part of the Union Gospel Mission. Why indeed. I mean, let's face it; you were in the Taj Mahal of treatment centers. The building was stunningly beautiful; new carpeting, cushy seating, nearly luxurious dormitory rooms; perfectly maintained grounds; and the food... I loved going there to visit you just so I could eat the latest chef creation in the cafeteria. I am not kidding. And of course the staff was topnotch. Yes, we, your parents, provided the best, and you rejected it. You were never happy there. And after forty-one days, you left.

Now you are at the Mission. The place is a bit worn and bedraggled. The residents are even more worn and bedraggled. You eat meals with your "brothers" at the Recovery Center, but you also eat with the homeless guys staying at the Mission. There are chores; your chore is to clean the chapel every morning. You tell me it can be a little scary to see what the homeless guys, the ones who sleep there overnight, leave behind.

And darn it if you aren't happy. Go figure. As Grandma asked, "Why do you suppose that is?"

I know why. Because you have never ever done anything the conventional way. Remember when you marched in the May Day parade as a kid, wearing huge cardboard boots that we had to strap to your waist? Don't suppose any of your schoolmates were doing that. How about circus school? While your peers were doing trampoline and trapeze, you were a clown. And wilderness camp? You were the only one there who was not Hmong. When those kids couldn't take the mosquitoes anymore, they all left! And you stayed at camp alone for the rest of the week. You loved it. You loved drawing. And make-believe. And vegetable gardening. And yo-yos. And winter camping. You never followed the crowd when it came to sports, Harry Potter, any kind of competition, computer games. You disliked them all.

You also love honesty and genuine people and kindness—all of which you get at the Mission. At first I asked, "Why here? What's different here from the Center?" Your response: "Because they treat me like a human being here." The genuine love seems to have touched you.

So, here you are doing your own thing, with other guys who seem to never have followed the straight and narrow path either. Or maybe they just got off the path along the way. You call each other "brother," and you support and teach each other, and clean the chapel. And that seems to be just what you need.

I suppose that is why you like it there. Thank God you do.

Love,
Mom

Day 38

Dear David,

Today someone I had not seen for over a year asked what I had been up to. I said, "I'm busy taking care of my family." She said, "Yes, but do you have a job?" To which I had to respond, "Well, sort of." Because being the mom of a child in full-blown addiction mode is a full-time job—a job for which I do not get paid, and for a long while, a job which had no reward.

For the past two years I've been checking out treatment centers; visiting you in treatment; consulting with doctors, counselors, and psychiatrists; taking you to appointments; researching sober houses; going to "I Am the Parent of an Addicted Child" meetings... you get the idea.

I am (mostly) happy to do all these things, because the reward has been your recovery. And if things go south again, I'll do them again.

But I do have to wonder, what do other parents do in their spare time?

Love,
Mom

Dear David,

"I'm praying for you." That's a phrase I hear from lots of people. In fact, sometimes I hear this sentiment from near-total strangers after they've heard of our trials. I wonder a lot about this statement.

First, I wonder, are you really praying for us? If so, I really appreciate you taking the time and effort to even think of us, much less taking the time to pray for us.

Then, sometimes, I think, are you saying that because you can't think of anything else to say? I mean, it is all so awful, what else can you say to fill the painful silence? I must admit, I sometimes say that to people in the midst of tragedy, just to assure them (and myself) that I am doing something.

Finally, I wonder, is this prayer going to help? Do you have a direct line to God? Does God have a quota, as in, he receives one hundred prayer requests for your sobriety, and then he grants it? What about the poor guy who has no one praying for him?

I admit, I have no answer to these questions. Prayer is a mystery to me. I do know that I pray, a lot, when times are bad, and even when times are good with you. I pray for others, although perhaps not as much as I should.

And I appreciate, really do appreciate, the prayers from others. Even if I do not know how it all works.

Love,
Mom

Dear David,

Here is a new word for you: *schadenfreude*. I've been hearing it a lot recently in radio interviews and seeing it in the newspaper. Here is what it means: "pleasure derived from the misfortunes of others." Now, who could possibly derive pleasure from the pain of others? Me, I tell you. And that is my deep, dark secret: ever since your troubles with addiction started, I feel pleasure when other families' seemingly perfect lives hit a bump in the road. How's that for honest? I am not proud.

Last night we had dinner with Danny and Jill. They have a seemingly perfect son and seemingly perfect family and seemingly perfect life... it's not hard to look pretty perfect when you compare it to the life our family has lived these past few years. Honestly, they don't mean to be perfect, it's just that things have turned out that way. And I am envious.

So, they were sharing that their son, Sam (you know, the one that you used to be such good friends with before your paths diverged radically), was actually struggling! His grades were slipping. He was spending too much time with friends, not enough time studying. Now this was not going to put an end to civilization, but it was causing them some consternation. I am ashamed and embarrassed to say that it was gratifying to see another parent fret over their son. I am not proud of this reaction.

I do not take pleasure in knowing that I take pleasure in the misfortunes of others. I am working on this "defect of character," as Al-Anon would say. Because, honestly, where does it get me? It sure doesn't change our family's misfortunes. And I do know that our fortunes are many.

I'm just letting you know that your mom is far from perfect. I guess you already knew that.

Love,
Mom

Day 42

Dear David,

Here's the thing: misery loves company. Or misery just needs company.

I was standing in the church office this morning, taking off my communion assistant robe. I saw John S., your friend and mine, who knows as much about misery as any of us. His son is in all kinds of trouble too. I asked him how it was going, and he started in about the latest painful episode, and we put our heads together and commiserated. In walked Jim, whom we barely know. Well, he heard talk of troubled sons, and that was all the prompting he needed; he started in with his story. Again, nothing new or shocking to John or me.

The point is, we could have continued that conversation, and the crowd would have kept growing and growing. We would've eventually had to move into a bigger space. Because we all have pain to share, especially when it comes to our teenage boys.

Misery does indeed love company. And while I'm sorry to hear the trials of other families, it is comforting to know that we're not alone.

Love,
Mom

Dear David,

Today I was cleaning out your closet. What a trip down memory lane that was. There was your box of rocks. Your *Yu-Gi-Oh!* cards. Your art supplies. Your camping gear.

All this brought a lump to my throat, not so much because it brought back fond memories, which it did, but because you don't use any of these things anymore.

You were always the kind of kid that jumped with gusto into any new project. And it was so much fun, I was happy to go along on the ride. Trips to art supply stores, *Yu-Gi-Oh!* tournaments, and Boy Scout meetings were a pleasure for me.

But soon you tired of each activity, and you jumped into the next.

I wonder if that was a sign of your addiction to come. After all, you were wildly enthusiastic about your drug of choice, and heaven knows you jumped right into that whole culture with gusto.

Only this time, it was not so easy to give it up.

I'm keeping your rocks and your drawing pads and all the other boyhood dreams that went with them. You may just come back to them. I hope so.

Love,
Mom

Day 45

Dear David,

I'm wondering if you can tell me where my iPad is. I've looked all over the house for days, actually weeks. It seems to have gone the way of your car keys...

So, have I reached the age where things just go missing? No. Not yet. It's just another vestige of your "using" days and all the insanity surrounding it.

You see, whenever you would show up after a long absence, Dad and I would use dark humor to lessen our anxiety. We would proclaim (to each other), "David's home; hide the silver!" We didn't do that literally, probably because we have no silver. But we were known to tuck a few things out of sight whenever you came around. We learned that lesson the hard way when the very few valuable things we owned suddenly went missing. You admitted later that you had stolen them to pay for your habit and your life on the streets.

Anyway, I am harkening back to the "Hide the silver!" days because I cannot find my darned iPad. I hid it when you came home a few months ago. Hid it too well. This past summer, I hid your car keys. Both sets. We have *never* found those, and it has been six months!

But that darned iPad. I admit, in my darker moments, I wonder if you hid it, along with the car keys, just to make me a little bit crazier than I already am thanks to your addiction.

It's all right. Time to come clean. Give me back my darned iPad. No questions asked.

As for the car keys, you can just throw those away. They are no use to us now, as your car is now sitting in a junkyard somewhere (you having totaled it).

One thing I'll say for sure: your life keeps us guessing and on our toes. And always looking.

Love you,
Mom

Day 48

Dear David,

Last night I went to the parent meeting at your old sober high school. Beth, the counselor, invited me to come. I figured, I'll take support wherever I can find it, and I really do mean that. It was a mostly unfamiliar group of parents, the old "I Am the Parent of an Addict" type of parents, some looking kind of stunned, most looking worn out from all this craziness. One woman talked about how she called the police for the first time last week. Another man was wondering if he should be honest about his own past drug use with his son. Someone else said, "Yes, our son is a senior, but he'll never graduate on time. Drugs took care of that." But we parents continue to show up week after week to get us through this painful saga. We sit in a circle, hopeful but cautious.

Then Beth turned to me and asked if I would be willing to share what has been going on with you since you graduated. I asked them how much time they had, which was followed by nervous laughter from the group, because they could tell some dreadful news was sure to follow. I tried to be brief, because, really no one wants to hear the bad stuff. We were sitting in that circle hoping for a slice of the good stuff. I told them how on the night after you graduated from high school (happiest day of my life, by the way), you disappeared, only to reappear every few days after that. I told them of the stints in treatment, the relapses, the arrest, the car accident, the night in the hospital. I didn't tell them about the lies, the thefts, or any of the details of your homelessness that I have gleaned from your stories. Then, with a sigh of relief from me and from my listeners, I was able to tell them that today, and for the past fourteen days, you have been at the Mission. That you are sober. That you are happy. That you are safe. So, they finally got to hear a slice of the "good."

Amid the stories of cops, and lies, and dropping out, there has to be that little slice. It's what keeps all of us parents coming to these difficult meetings, much as we'd rather be doing something—anything—else.

Next month, I pray that I'll still be among the featured "life is good" speakers. But I look around, and I know that I may not be. It's still all so precarious, isn't it?

Love,
Mom

Day 52

Dear David,

Of course you'll notice I haven't written for a while. No more frantic missives from me; I worry, but I'm not obsessed. Actually, I feel pretty good about where you're at.

You are at the Mission. Less than cushy accommodations; less than gourmet meals; no fancy doctors, psychologists, "treatment specialists," or psychiatrists—just real men who have a deep need to get clean and sober, and are willing to do anything to get there. And they all rely on each other and on God. They are not afraid to say so. And that is very genuine. Just as you like it.

Tonight I will be joining you at "Sing-Along," which happens every Wednesday night at the Mission. At that time, all the brothers and their families and alumni, and anyone else who loves to sing and loves the Mission, gather in the dingy meeting room. The band plays their guitars and drums and piano. The words to songs like "Will the Circle Be Unbroken?" and "I'll Fly Away" are displayed using an old overhead projector, and we all sing.

This has taken me a few weeks to get used to. The first time we went, Dad in his button down Lands' End shirt, me in my cute khaki Dockers, we were a little uncomfortable. A lot uncomfortable. Let's just say that I now don my old, familiar jeans and sneakers, just so I fit in. The singing was a little intimidating too. So while Dad has taken "a pass" on the sing-along, preferring to take you out to dinner on a different night instead, I have grown to relish it.

The singing is great fun, but even more so, it's genuine and from the heart. These guys are really celebrating the spirit that dwells in this place and within them.

So, save me a chair beside you. Tonight we sing.

Love,
Mom

Day 53

Dear David,

Yesterday you told me the most shocking news, and I've been thinking about it all day. You told me that one of your "brothers," Scott, walked away. Just gathered up a few things and walked out of the Mission.

I really, really liked Scott. In these first thirty days, during which you are not allowed to go anywhere without a brother in tow, Scott willingly sat in the backseat of our car as I drove you to doctor's appointments. He sat in waiting rooms with me, chatting and paging through outdated, irrelevant magazines.

He was nice looking, well dressed, and always friendly. He told me about his five-year-old son. He told me how this was the second time he was at the Mission. He declared, "I'll take my time. I'm in no hurry. I'm going to get it right this time." He had an easy laugh, and he loved to joke with the two of us.

So now you've told me that all anyone saw was Scott walking away with the hood of his sweatshirt pulled over his head, and a backpack on his back. His roommate told you he had packed up his baseball cards and his signed baseball, which nearly brought me to tears. To think that these men still have the presence of mind to carry around their special treasures with them as they venture out into the cruel world. Almost like a little boy carries around his Matchbox cars, even as he knows he'll get beat up on the way to school.

I feel sad for Scott. I pray daily, hourly, for Scott.

I asked you, "You wouldn't walk away, would you?" You rolled your eyes, "No, Mom." If nothing else, I know the looming Minnesota winter keeps you from walking out the door into the streets. But surely there is something more that keeps you there.

Scott makes me aware how fragile this thing called recovery can be, and what a perilous journey you and all your brothers have ahead of you.

I thank God you found the Mission. And I thank God that you are staying put.

Love,
Mom

Day 54

Dear David,

Here is one great benefit to recovery: you let me touch you! How incredible is that? You of the shrugging shoulder, the wince, the shudder whenever anyone tried to touch you... you are now willing to tolerate human contact!

You even let me kiss your cheek. You allow me to hug you. Oh my, how I have missed your sweet little boy embrace!

I don't know why this has happened, but I am giddy. To be able to hug you hello or kiss you good-bye is happiness beyond measure.

Recovery must make you feel lovable again.

Love,
Mom

Day 56

Dear David,

The other day you told me that you thought of Mrs. G. as a "second mom." To which I replied, "REALLY?" I didn't actually say that out loud. I just nodded and screamed it inside my head.

This woman who let you live with her in the throes of your addiction? The one who bailed you out when we didn't want you bailed out? The one who called me and said, "I'm letting him live with me until things cool down." REALLY?

OK, I guess I should thank her for housing you and feeding you when you wouldn't go to treatment. Maybe. But didn't her "kindness" just prolong the agony?

And may I just say, was Mrs. G. there when you were colicky, when you were in the hospital, when the kids were bullying you in school, when you had to go to endless dreadful hours of speech therapy? I didn't think so.

So, you may call her a nice lady, an enabler, a pal. But don't be giving me this "second mom" shit.

Love,
(Your real) Mom

Day 58

Dear David,

Here is the difficult part about being a parent. No, scratch that. Here is one of the many, many difficult parts about being a parent. They call it "detachment" or "letting him make his own mistakes" or "letting him feel his own pain," and on and on. Some people call it a fine line; I call it a canyon. That leap I need to take from nurturing you, loving you, and protecting you from the bad guys, to letting you figure this out on your own. And it seems there are just so few steps to get there. One minute you are a baby and I have you bundled you up 'til you sweat, because no cold air will touch my baby; the next you are calling me from the Mission, complaining about how much you hate it there and they aren't fair, and no one is compassionate... Well, what's a mom to do? I did as I was taught, saying, "Sounds like you're feeling pretty frustrated." And in the meantime the tiger mama inside of me is looking for a way to kill one or two of these guys that broke your heart. Sorry, just being honest. I know that I'm not supposed to murder anyone that hurts your feelings;

I'm not supposed to solve these problems for you. And, let me tell you, any mother will tell you this is darn near impossible. Because I have had a *ton* of practice protecting you—from cold winds, mean teachers, bullying classmates, and all the pain that came with the depression and anxiety inside of you.

But the wise ones out there tell me I am done protecting you. I should listen. I should "mirror" your feelings, as in, "Sounds like you're feeling..." To which you rightly respond, "OH, DO YOU THINK SO*?!*" Listen, kid, I'm just doing what the books tell me.

The books and my wise friends say you will figure it out on your own. And a certain amount of complaining and gnashing of teeth is all just part of the package. I just wish you would gnash your teeth with someone else. Because, honestly, I carry it all in my heart and in my gut.

I try this mirroring technique on myself: "Sounds like I'm feeling frustrated. Or maybe desperate." Honestly, it doesn't make me feel any better.

So, I pray. I actually read a prayer this morning, which I think I'll keep in my pocket. It said, "Cause my son to call out to You in his distress and confusion. Cause him to seek You with abandon." I like that; call God instead of me.

I love you, and on the day of your birth I promised to always protect you. Now it's time for you and God to figure out how this protection goes. I really am trying to let you do this without Mom's help.

Love you,
Mom

Dear David,

Today I talked to a woman, Carolyn, at church. She said, "I read your blog every day. And the amazing thing to me is you always bounce right back!"

She's right. We have hit some pretty hard times, you and me. Yet I've lived to tell about it.

I do think I have some optimism in my nature. And some faith that God will put all this right.

Really, what choice do I have? Wallow in misery and doom? Or still hold out some hope that we'll get through this?

I choose to hope. And bounce back after every fall.

Love you,
Mom

Dear David,

Yesterday as we were driving in the van, on our way to a doctor's appointment, I had to wonder, whose life is this anyway?

Because you are still "on probation" at the Mission, we have to take a brother with us for every outing. Yesterday, it was Rob. Sweet, jovial, LOUD Rob. He asked if we could pick up Bonnie, his "friend." Well, she lives in the female version of the Mission. So, here we are driving around town, Rob yammering on about all manner of topics, and Bonnie with her pink and purple hair, playing a very noisy game on her phone. I thought, "How did this happen? How did this middle-class mom end up with her young wayward son in the front seat of her van, and two formerly homeless addicts in the backseat?" Nothing in my previous life prepared me for this. Then again, nothing in my previous life prepared me for treatment centers, trauma units, ambulances, police, jail, bail, and public defenders either.

So, at first I was pretty taken aback. I mean, really? You had to invite someone who you later told me has spent more time in jail than out of jail in his life? And he had to invite his girlfriend who clearly has had some pretty rough times of her own, being that she only sees her children, who live with her aunt, every other weekend?

Yes, I have to admit, I am a snob. A white, upper-middle-class snob. One whose life may have been somewhat challenging at times, but nothing like this. I mean, did I really want to invite this element of society into the back of my van?

Well, of course God and you (unwittingly) had something to teach me. Because these two people were just so darn happy to be riding in the backseat. They were thrilled to be going to the Dollar Store, where Rob could get another set of headphones ("I want the red ones!") for ten dollars. Rob laughed as we passed a store where he had been caught stealing as a young boy, saying, "They asked me if I wanted them to call my parents or call the cops. I said, 'Call the cops! Please! Nothing could be as bad as my parents when they find out.'" Bonnie and Rob (I know, it does remind one of *Bonnie and Clyde*, doesn't it?) were just all around happy to be alive. And they seemed so like innocent children, riding home from school in the backseat of my van.

At one point on our venture, Rob said, "Yah, Bonnie likes to collect rocks. She likes to get them all cleaned up and shiny. She wants a machine that can do that." You said, "You mean a rock tumbler?" "Yeah. I tell her she can just use an old toothbrush and nail polish remover." Well, it was all I could do not to turn the car around and take them to Target and buy her a rock tumbler for about fifteen dollars. Bonnie would have gone home thinking she'd won the lottery. And I wouldn't even have noticed the deficit in my bank account.

David, I'm coming to find out, there are all kinds of people in this world. And we are surely not above them. And joy is where you find it. Like in a ten-dollar set of red headphones. Or a fifteen-dollar rock tumbler. Maybe we'll go get one on our next outing.

I've got a lot to learn.

Love,
Mom

Day 62

Dear David,

It's been a few days since I've written. As you know, I was in Wausau because Grandma Jean was having heart surgery. I gotta say, it was a pretty rough event. Grandpa and I had to keep reminding ourselves and each other that she is an eighty-four-year-old woman with Parkinson's disease, so recovery is bound to be rough. But I tell you, nothing prepares a person for sitting in a folding chair for three days, in a hospital room with no window, watching your mother sleep, head dangling, mouth wide open. Every time I stood to leave, wishing I could finally find a decent cup of coffee, another health worker came in. Shouts of "JEAN, WAKE UP!" will forever ring in my head. She did not wake up. At one point a physical therapist actually put her on an exercise bike. I swear to God he must have had to tape her hands on to the handles. She "pedaled," as she sat there with her eyes closed and mouth open, while he moved the handles back and forth, yammering on and on. Yesterday, just as I was leaving and Aunt Julie was entering, she woke up! So, she'll be fine.

There were moments of humor, which you of all people would have appreciated. When the chaplain came in and asked if she would like a prayer shawl, Grandma whispered, "Yes." The chaplain asked Grandma her favorite color. Grandma said violet! Violet? Grandpa and I were stunned. I said, "Really, her favorite color is violet?" Grandpa said, "That's news to me. And even if it were, I think she would have said purple. But violet?" Here's the hilarious part: that chaplain came back three minutes later with a violet prayer shawl. Don't you suppose that she has had this violet prayer shawl sitting in the bottom of the pile for about two years? She finally got a taker! And Grandma has a violet prayer shawl... her favorite color.

So, what did this weekend have to do with you? You and I (and your sister) share the same sense of humor about things like this. You would have immediately understood the hilarity of the violet shawl, and the physical therapist propping a near-comatose Grandma on a recumbent bike. This weekend made me miss you fiercely.

Of course the good news is I will talk to you (and see you!) very soon, I hope.

Love,
Mom

Day 65

Dear David,

So, we got a great phone call from you this weekend! Much to your surprise, you received your thirty-day medallion! Now, this was not a surprise to me. Believe me, this mother has counted every single day. One more day of you being safe and sober and me being able to sleep at night is just an incredible blessing.

You were very happy when they surprised you with the medallion. And why shouldn't you be happy? You've worked hard for this. But then, when they said to you, "Tell us how you did it," you replied, "I don't know. I just did what they told me to do." At first I was a little frustrated that you didn't give yourself credit for the hard work you did—physically (cleaning the chapel every day) and emotionally and spiritually... all those meetings!

But it really was just as you said. You did what you were told to do. Yet there is something more. The work you have done is to let the good spirit of recovery in. You have looked for miracles, sought out fellowship, asked questions, and prayed. You've probably done a whole lot more than that. You said to me, "I've gotten plenty of thirty-day medallions. But this one feels different."

This time is different for me too. It feels more honest. It feels like you are taking ownership a whole lot more than before. It feels hopeful. Well, a little hopeful. Because we can't help but worry and wonder, based on past experience.

Just for today, you are truly on the right path. I'm working on trusting a little bit more every day that this will continue. The trust is getting easier.

I am so proud of you. All the work you have done. And all the good work you have allowed to be done in you.

Let's keep going on this path of recovery.

Love you,
Mom

Day 67

Dear David,

Well, you called again last night, and much to our delight, we learned you've been sprung! That is, after thirty days at the Mission, you are allowed to leave for a few hours at a time, *without a brother*. So you are coming home for dinner tonight. And I am beside myself with joy and excitement. We've invited Auntie and Ellen. We will finally dine as a family; something we have not done for many, many months.

I do have to admit, I am pretty darn anxious. I feel like Martha in the Bible, running around busying herself, making sure your room looks exactly right, hoping I cook exactly the right foods and say exactly the right things. Pacing and planning; "Will he want to play a card game? How about a movie? Will he want to be alone?" It's as if I need to make the night perfect... otherwise, you could bolt. Or, rather, you will want to bolt.

But, I know this is not the way it should be. Not the way you want it to be. We are not on probation after all, are we? Dad assures me that you want to be here with us. And if you can't be here, if you need to leave, it won't be because I didn't choose the right ice cream, or find the right show on TV. It will be because of something that is going on with you, something you have to deal with, demons and all. "Try not to take it as rejection of *you*," he says. Fat chance.

But I do try. Today I will cook and clean (although you won't notice that), and just generally be thrilled that you're going to be sitting and eating with us. And if it's a great time, then great. If it's not a great time, then there will always be another opportunity. At least that's what I tell myself. One day at a time, right, kid?

So, hurry on home. I can hardly wait.

Love you,
Mom

Day 68

Dear David,

Well, it was just plain wonderful to have you with us.

Although things have gotten a little rough for you lately at the Mission, I still feel confident that you will succeed. You'll find a way to make it work. And I couldn't be more proud of you.

I was just so happy to see your smiling face and hug you tight. And I could tell you were happy to see us, although you were even happier to see Chester and Patch... that's all right; I miss the animals when I'm away from home too!

Love you,
Mom

Day 72

Dear David,

I get it about recovery, I really do. You're doing the best you can. And easy does it, and one day at a time, and live and let live.

But here's the deal. Sometimes you just do something for someone. No matter if it feels exactly comfortable or not. Case in point: going to church with your mom. You know it's important to her. Not to mention the fact that she has been to HELL AND BACK doing things she didn't want to be doing as a result of your addiction and recovery.

So, really? You can't get yourself out of bed to go to church, sit through a sermon for an hour, and crawl back home?

All is not perfect in the land of recovery.

Sometimes you just do something for someone else.

Love you anyway,
Mom

Day 75

Dear David,

I'm writing this one day after our sweet dog Chester died. This is so painful; I feel as if I am going to break into a million little pieces. Chester came into our lives when you were in kindergarten. You grew up with him. And he saw us through all the good times and the bad. He was a constant, unconditionally loving companion.

Christine drove from Sioux Falls when we told her the news that Chet was sick. You came home from the Mission. The four of us were together to say good-bye.

As you said, the blessing of the event was that Chester was able to bring the four of us—you, me, Dad, and Christine—together. It had been a very long time since we could be together without tension, tears, and rancor. We were together in sadness, but also in peace.

This past year has been so darn painful for this family. You were right to remind me to look for the miracles in it all.

I'm trying.

Love,
Mom

Day 81

Dear David,

Well, it has been one tough week. Who knew a dog could have such a profound impact on one's life? (Or, more accurately, the absence of a dog.) Sympathetic listeners tell me "he was part of the family," which indeed he was. But more than that, he was part of the fabric of this household. His toys, his blankets, his presence are in every room. The silence is, in fact, deafening. Certain areas of the room are off-limits to me; I cannot lie down on the couch, because of course that is where he would snuggle with me. I ask myself, "How could the mail have come already, and I didn't know it?" Of course, my barking alarm is no longer here.

When you talk to me, you ask me how I am doing. I tell you about my sadness and my fear that I will never get over this pain. You tell me I am going to be all right. And when I ask you if you think I will feel this way forever, you say, firmly, "No." But, really, how would you know? Perhaps because you have been through a lot of awful pain yourself, and it has ended. Or at least diminished. Or changed. For today.

Tonight I am going to a "pet loss support group," which actually sounds a little pathetic. That's a pretty arrogant thing for me to be saying, actually, since I have been walking around weeping all week. And while I've been complaining about being an unwilling member of the "I Am the Parent of an Addicted Child" Club, now I can add "I Am the Parent of a Deceased Dog" member to my titles.

I do want you to know that yesterday I was actually feeling a little better. I don't think I even cried when I *didn't* hear Chester at the door.

So, perhaps you are right. I am sure you are right. I won't feel this way forever. Just as there was hope with you, and I continue to feel hope for you, surely there is hope with the loss of our beloved Chester.

Love,
Mom

Day 82

Dear David,

OK, so things have been a little tough lately—Chester dying, Grandma Jean having an incredibly difficult recovery from surgery, Grandpa Don dying. And then there's you and your up-and-down recovery. I've been sad; I've been overwhelmed. And I think, "Now just how much more can a person take?"

I want to tell you about two stories I have come across lately. The first is from a book I am reading, a memoir. The author is a guy who grew up with an awful father, and pretty much had a dreadful childhood, but still managed to get it all together to be happy and married and a successful author and a professor of surgery at Yale. Anyway, the opening quote to his book is: "Be kind, for everyone you meet is fighting a great battle." I really like that. I mean, there are times I really want to hang a sign around my neck letting everyone know that I am a very put-upon person, and you'd better be nice to me. Then I read this quote and I think, "Well, everybody has their sorrow, I guess."

Here is the second story. For this class I'm taking, I had to interview one of my classmates. I did not know this woman at all; she lives in Madison, Wisconsin. We were randomly paired, and interviewed each other over the phone. Anyway, I read Sharon's "biography," the little description of ourselves that we posted online for the others taking this class. Her biography told of how, for twenty years, she has suffered from excruciating pain, headaches, and even bouts of passing out! It turns out that the pain is being caused by the effects of some faulty orthodontia she had as a teen, and for which she is now just getting treatment. So, we started talking about how we deal with pain in our lives, and she mentioned that she had a ton of therapy a few years back because HER FATHER WAS MURDERED. Get this: her dad was living his dream in Palm Springs. Some drug addicts stabbed him, LEFT HIM IN THE DESERT, and kind of casually moved into his house.

So, I think, "OK. My life has surely been tough lately, and I'm pretty sick of it. But maybe I don't need to hang a sign around my neck. Perhaps everyone is fighting their own great battles, just like me."

One more thing I wanted to mention: I heard an interview on the radio a few years ago with Elaine Stritch, who was a comedian. She said, "Everybody's got a sack of rocks," meaning of course that everyone is living with some kind of burden.

Now, my sack of rocks has been pretty darn heavy lately. And I'll surely hope for something lighter in 2015, but I am reminded that we're all suffering. And we all have each other. I need my family, my hope, and my faith in God. And it really does help to know that everybody's got a sack of rocks.

Love you,
Mom

Day 84

Dear David,

You've talked about triggers before. Those seemingly innocuous things that make you want to start using again.

And I think I know exactly what you mean.

Last Sunday our family was riding home from a long weekend out of town. You started texting the minute we put on our seat belts. The texting lasted the whole hour and a half home. Your sister looked at me. I knew what she was thinking. She knew what I was thinking.

After we arrived home, and you ran upstairs to TEXT SOME MORE, Christine turned to me and said, "He's acting suspicious," to which I could only agree.

Texting is just one of the triggers this family has. Things that make us worry and wonder, could you be using again?

Love,
Mom

Day 86

Dear David,

Well, that was a very dark night. Just how did that happen?

There you were at the Mission. Doing just plain great. Making connections. Finding a sponsor, staying sober. Then, like a flash, we seem to be right back where we started. The lies, the fears, the chaos.

It started with your arrival home. We were very surprised to see you walk in the door. Without warning, you informed us that you had been granted a "family pass." I say "without warning" because first, we did not expect it, and second, hindsight tells us we surely did need a warning. We were not prepared.

Like many bad things, it started off so right. You were busy making plans to go to a meeting with Ari, an old friend from treatment days. You told us she was sober and "doing really well." OK, so far, so good. Then the descent begins.

You can't get a hold of Ari. You do get a hold of Ari. Ari can't go to the meeting. Not now, anyway. Ari is going to get back to you. Ari still hasn't gotten back to you. On and on it goes. Back and forth. Back and forth. That old, gut-wrenching, frantic tapping of the laptop keys... you're looking for something. I ask what you're searching for. You say, "A meeting." Like you don't already know where and when all of the St. Paul AA meetings are. Texting takes over. A whole lot of texting... more than is warranted for a simple get-together with Ari. Dad and I have plans to go out. We leave you behind, me knowing for sure that something bad is brewing.

When we returned, there was the old familiar note on the kitchen counter: "I'm out with Ari. Don't worry. I am safe. I love you." Oh boy, the code words, "I am safe," which mean "I am out doing things I should not be doing."

I told Dad you were out getting into trouble. He, always the optimist when it comes to you, denied it. But I've been through this script with you before.

The next morning you showed up at our door at eight o'clock. I was at church. You told Dad that you had spent the night at the Mission and took the bus from there to return home just then. Incredulously, I asked Dad, "Really? He took the bus at this hour of the morning?" Dad just so wanted to believe you. Ha. You are not fooling me.

That night, you fessed up. You had been out all night with Ari. And some of your other old pals. Drugs were present; you claimed that you refused them. I don't know. I do not want to know. I have heard all that I need to hear.

I told Dad to put you in the car and drive you back to the Mission. He did. I told Dad not to expect that you would be staying at the Mission. I recognized your tone of voice, the look on your face, the signs that tell me you are going to bolt. Dad wasn't so sure. Ha!

Well, we can either thank God, or we can thank the cold Minnesota winter, but you stayed that night at the Mission. And you are still there. You called to apologize the next night. You said, "This is not who I want to be." Indeed.

So, we are left shaken and off balance. Like you got to the cliff and God's hand pulled you back before you jumped.

Whew.

Love,
Mom

Day 90

Dear David,

Today I am writing you from the skilled nursing facility in Appleton. This is where Grandma is recovering from her surgery. My job seems to be sitting and listening to her talk, responding as necessary, and watching her sleep. She sleeps a lot. In fact, I have renamed this place "Elsa's House of Sleep." There used to be a business in St. Paul by that name. It may still exist. I remember seeing it on a sign, and I just loved the sound of that name. Anyway, I call it the "House of Sleep" because its very air induces sleep. The moment I walk in, my eyelids get heavy. Yesterday, after all the therapies (occupational, physical, and speech) were over, Grandma fell asleep in the recliner and I curled up on her bed! I was a little embarrassed when the aide entered the room and for a split second seemed to be wondering which of us was the patient!

Grandma is at lunch now; I'll finish this letter to you before I nod off.

I haven't seen you since Thanksgiving. And didn't we have a good time? Your friend Kevin from the Mission and Dad, Christine, Auntie, and Ellen were all there. We ate well, played games, and you even joined us at church a few days later! It went really well, although I still found it pretty difficult. Trust seems to be in short supply for me these days.

Just the weekend before, you had gone AWOL, and I'm pretty sure we nearly lost you to the streets again. You came back to the Mission on Sunday night, thank God, and things were fine again. And yet... for me there is always the wondering, "Will this be the weekend he disappears?"

Dad gets mad at me for talking this way. He says I have to appreciate the good and quit worrying about the bad. He is right of course, but, let's face it: there has been plenty of bad to keep me on my toes.

Honestly, I am so thankful for our time this Thanksgiving. I am so proud and so pleased that you are sober. I'm happy that I got to "show you off" at church. It is amazing the amount of attention you garner just by showing up.

I'm praying to be able to trust again. But I'm always cautious.

Grandma is back from lunch. Time to curl up for a nap at Elsa's.

Love,
Mom

Day 91

Dear David,

Last night, at an "I Am the Parent of an Addicted Child" meeting, Dad talked to the mom of one of your former cohorts at the Center. Dad asked how Melissa was doing. The mom said, "Great! She's at the program in Long Beach, California, and she's doing really well!"

I'd like to say, who wouldn't be doing well in Long Beach, California? I mean, couldn't we all just use a break on the beach, soaking up California sun?

But I won't say it. That would not be kind. Still. I am thinking it.

Love,
Mom

Dear David,

As I mentioned earlier, a few nights ago Dad went to an "I Am the Parent of an Addicted Child" meeting. As you know, I was busy snoozing at Elsa's House of Sleep. This particular group meets once a month. Each time they have featured presenters, parents of an addicted child who have been through the wringer, seen it all, and pretty much come out whole on the other end. Anyway, last night's presenters told their journey of their son's drug use. How it ended up in heroin addiction.

And then he died. Not quite the ending the group had expected, or certainly hoped for.

I'm glad I didn't go.

Love you,
Mom

Dear David,

This weekend, at the end of an especially strained visit to our house, you pulled me aside. You asked, "Are you in therapy?"

OK, I could have taken this question a whole lot of ways. Like, "I'm concerned about you. This addiction and recovery and all it entails must be really hard for you. I hope you're getting help because this must be really painful, and you deserve some relief."

Or I could have taken it as: "Things are really not going well. You are yelling. I am yelling. I hope you are in therapy because clearly this is your fault and you better get yourself fixed."

I of course chose the latter interpretation, because I was just so mad.

For the record, I *am* in therapy. Every week I talk about you. And me. And our crazy, crazy family. And I sure as hell hope you're in therapy too.

Because you're just as crazy and damaged as I am.

Love,
Mom

Day 95

Dear David,

I wonder if you've heard about Pavlov and his dogs. A long time ago, a Russian scientist by the name of Ivan Pavlov was looking at how dogs salivate in response to being fed. I know, kind of odd, but somebody has to study these things. Anyway, he accidentally discovered that the dogs would begin to salivate whenever he entered the room. His entrance was a trigger; the dogs realized that when he came in, they were going to get fed, so they automatically started salivating. Thus was born the term *conditioned response*, or *Pavlovian response*.

I tell you all this because like Pavlov's dogs, I have noticed that I have a conditioned response to many of your actions. These responses arose from living with you in your "bad days."

Here are some sounds or actions that elicit panic and dread from this mother:

> • The sound of you stuffing a backpack
> • The sound and sight of you typing away on your laptop

- The sight of you on your cell phone
- The sound of you saying that you're going to take the bus to your destination even after being offered a car ride
- The sight of a note saying that you're out with friends. (If the note says "I am safe," I know you are not.)
- The sound of you upstairs in your room for an extended period of time
- The sound of you asking if you can take your laptop with you to your new home. (Let's just say many a fine electronic device has disappeared from this house.)
- The sound of you asking if you can borrow a few bucks to go to a movie

Now, on the surface, these are very benign activities. And now that you're sober, they should return to their benign states.

But just like the dogs, I have been conditioned. I get on high alert, asking you just who you are texting, what you are frantically searching for on your laptop, what you are packing in your backpack as you leave the house.

And like a good recovering person, you answer politely. You reassure me. You ask if I would like to check your backpack, to which I reply, "Good God, no. Never again do I want to search through a backpack!"

You ask me how you can help me feel more comfortable, and I don't have any ideas.

Your past life was so frightening to me; I am on constant high alert.

I just wanted to tell you, and I have told you in person, that this is really difficult for me. I love you and I trust you on an intellectual level. But on a gut level, I just can't. You tell me you understand.

I pray that someday this can change.

In the meantime, I remain your ever-loving mom.

Love,
Mom

THE SOBER HOUSE

Day 102

Dear David,

Well, it has been one week since you moved out of the Mission and into your new home. You are now happily residing in a sober house with nine other men. You're happy because these men are much younger than the men at the Mission, you get to work, you get to go to the AA meetings you really like, and most of all, I am convinced, you get your beloved cell phone back (just kidding... sort of).

Really, this is a good and brave move for you to have made. Leaving the Mission was scary in some ways for you. You didn't want to fail; you didn't want to be judged. But you prayed on it, and it seemed like the right thing to do.

I myself have hardly told a soul. Because like all things that have to do with you and your recovery, I rejoice in the victories, but I also hold my breath, afraid to trust the process.

I do believe that just as the Mission was the right place, the best place, for you a few months ago, so this sober house really does feel like the best place for you now.

I feel truly grateful for all that God has provided for you and us and our recovery. Let's keep it going.

Love,
Mom

Day 104

Dear David,

I was talking to Pastor Lois today about your (and therefore my) troubles. She suggested I talk to Jennifer, a member of our church, whose son is suffering from an addiction to video games. Video games? What's next?

Soon I was directed to another church mom, Samantha. Her son is addicted to internet gambling. I tell you, you boys will glom on to just about anything, won't you? It's enough to break your mothers' hearts. And it does.

Love you,
Mom

Day 106

Dear David,

Really? That's the best you can do? After all the recovery and the meetings and heartfelt conversation... that's the best you can do for a Saturday night?

I speak, of course, of your latest escapade with Joe. Let's see, you know a multitude of men living at your sober house, a mob of men from the Mission, a gaggle of guys from all the AA meetings you attend. You wanted to see a movie, and you wanted a friend to go with you. So, who do you walk in the door with on Saturday? Joe. That's right. The same person you were arrested with, the one you spent the night in jail with in Waterloo, Iowa. The one who was riding in the car when you hit the utility pole. The one who you lived with after we kicked you out. Really?

Joe is a nice enough guy. But, honestly, the nerve you had bringing him into our house was downright galling. I mean, haven't we had enough trauma in our days?

You told me you guys were headed down to the gas station to buy candy. I'll bet. Pardon me for being cynical and angry.

Let's talk about making better choices, shall we?

Love anyway,
Mom

Dear David,

Last night Dad went to an "I Am the Parent of an Addicted Child" meeting. Here is the story he brought home; another sad one.

This couple put their son in treatment for heroin addiction. Then they went on vacation! Probably a very well-deserved vacation. All the parents know that feeling... first good night's sleep in months, probably years. Anyway, this couple gets home from their trip. They box up a "care package"... you know, a bunch of stuff people in treatment appreciate receiving from the "outside." I can imagine their glee as they packed up the candy, the magazines, the cookies. Then, they drove over to the treatment center. Their son was gone. He had walked off. Now, isn't that one of the saddest stories you have ever heard?

Dad talked to them afterward. He said, "You must have been crushed." He tells me they almost lit up with recognition of the feeling. "Yes," they said. "That is actually it. We were crushed."

Geez, I know that feeling. I don't feel it now, but I sure have been crushed. Crushed by despair and sadness when the rug of optimism and hope was pulled out from under me. All the parents in this sad yet hopeful group have felt crushed at one time or another.

I really don't have much more to say about it, except I can't stop picturing this newly tanned and smiling couple carrying their treasure box, only to be turned away. It breaks my heart.

So glad you're doing fine these days.

Love you,
Mom

Day 109

Dear David,

There's a weird feature I get with our cell phone company's "family plan." Every Monday morning I receive an e-mail from them. The subject line says, "Weekly Update: David's been receiving picture messages during your late night hours. See more..." As if I want to see more. But, there it is: line after line describing "David's week." Thirty-six contacts. Five hundred and fifty text messages. Twelve picture messages, two at night! If I move fast enough, I can delete the message. But usually, I scroll down to peek... and see the awful news.

Now why does Verizon think I want to see such incriminating evidence? I mean, really, I do not need to know that my son is receiving "picture messages" at 2:30 in the morning! Or that he has texted some unknown number 385 times!

It's probably all innocent fun. Pictures from a friend at the beach! Funny animal shots!

I don't know. I don't need to know. I certainly do not want to know. I heard way too many sordid stories during your "using" days; I don't need evidence from the phone company to help me invent even more.

I used to get these updates every day. I've been able to change the settings so that I get them only once a week. I am working on getting them to stop entirely. Clearly, no one at this company has a child suffering from addiction and all the awful stuff that brings into a family's life.

In the meantime, I'll keep trying to delete the messages before I take a peek. I'm trying.

Love you,
Mom

Dear David,

This is the time of year when I normally send out Christmas cards. I should be doing that again this year, but it all feels a little awkward. What would I say?

Dear Friends,

Here's a recap of our year. After months of drug abuse, our son David went to outpatient treatment. David walked out. We don't know where he went, but it sure wasn't home. David went to inpatient treatment. David walked out. David lived on the streets for weeks. Our daughter, Christine, attended four weeks of partial hospitalization for depression. We had to give away our cat, Finn, whom we had loved for two and a half years, because he was attacking Patch, our other cat. John's dad died. David continued to use and live on the streets. David got arrested in Iowa after his grandpa's funeral, for speeding and driving under the influence. David spent the night in jail in Iowa. Someone else's mother bailed him out. David totaled his car. David was saved by the Mission. Martha's mom had heart surgery, from which she is having a hell of a time recovering. Our beloved dog Chester died. David left the Mission, but not to return to the streets (thank God for Minnesota winters!). He lives in a sober house, and at the time of this writing, he remains sober.

Merry Christmas, and for God's Sake, let's have a Happy New Year!

Kind of makes you want to turn the letter over for some better news, doesn't it?

Don't worry; I won't mail it.

Love you,
Mom

Day 111

Dear David,

I'm not proud to admit this, but these Christmas letters we keep receiving are making me just a tad bitter. I read the notes about kids starring in plays, making the dean's list (again), and lobbying for world peace. I'm happy for these families. Mostly. But I want to ask them, "Do you have any idea what hardship is?" It sounds like resentment, which of course it is.

So this year I will not write a letter. I mean, who wants to hear about addiction, homelessness, death of a parent, and loss of a pet?

Now that I have that out of my system, I will say this: we are blessed beyond measure. And it really is beyond measure. We cannot quantify the gratitude we have for your recovery; the gratitude for Grandpa Don and his life; the gratitude we have for our dog and cat who gave us such unconditional love. It is kind of hard to put in a letter, I guess… especially when you are competing with letters that are so filled with external accomplishments. But we really have learned what counts.

So I won't put it on paper, beyond what I have written to you. But it is in my heart.

I am so thankful for the family we have, for the path we have been shown.

And, honestly, I *am* happy for the families who have had so much happiness of their own this year.

Merry Christmas, my sweet boy. So glad you are here with us to celebrate.

Love,
Mom

Day 113

Dear David,

On Christmas Eve you were an acolyte. You and your cousin Ellen were acolytes for the 8:00 p.m. service at church, just as you were last year.

You two were so cute and sweet, it nearly did me in. You holding the cross, Ellen holding the Bible, chatting and laughing away in the back of the church, waiting for the procession to begin. I was the lector, so I got to witness it all, the two of you in your white robes, smiling and teasing each other. Every once in a while you would call me over to let me in on the joke. Just like last year, before things had all gone wrong.

It seemed like old times could in fact now be our new times. I sure hope so.

Afterward, I told you how proud and pleased I was to see you as an acolyte. I told you that I'd like to think you did it for me. You paused, as I knew you would, because in fact you didn't do it for me. You weren't quite sure just how or why you were once again signed up to be an acolyte. (I signed you up, but only after getting permission from you!) I told you to just go with it, to agree that you had done it for me.

And you did. You told me you did it for me. And I thanked you.

And don't I deserve it? One great big night of joy seeing my boy up there in a white robe holding the cross? Indeed I do. Indeed we all do.

We're praying for a happy New Year. A year filled with all the promise that a smiling boy with a cross and a laughing girl with a Bible can bring.

Love you,
Mom

Day 114

Dear David,

Here is another thing I noticed when you were acolyting on Christmas Eve: your shoes.

Underneath your white robe, your big scuffed athletic shoes peeked out from under your robe.

I had asked you earlier to change your shoes, to wear something a tad bit dressier for Christmas Eve. You of course would not. Who was going to see them? Well, everyone.

I sat in the front of the church, wincing at those big untied Nikes.

But a few things did occur to me.

First, you were there. You were sober. You were an acolyte. An acolyte who just happened to be wearing the wrong footwear.

Second, you looked like my little boy. The one who rebelled and said, "I can wear what I want!," which indeed you did and still do now. And I love that child.

So, when I turned to Pastor Javen, sitting next to me in the pew, and whispered, "We really did try to get him to wear different shoes," and he answered, "It's all right," I knew he was, in fact, so right.

Love,
Mom

Day 116

Dear David,

Today someone forwarded me an article that had the subtitle "No one brings dinner when your daughter is an addict," and I thought, "Boy, oh boy, don't I know it." Sure, they'll bring casseroles when you are in the middle of chemo, but comfort food when your son has disappeared due to addiction? I think not. Addiction is a terrible disease, yet no one seems to know what to do for a family when it hits.

But then in the next hour I received a comment on Facebook. Someone was responding to a picture I had posted. You and Ellen were all smiles; you were acolytes for the Christmas Eve service. The person said, "Those smiles make me smile. Happiness will wind its way back to all of you, and I am so glad that David is working hard to make it happen for himself. I BELIEVE." And I thought, "Well, yes, I believe too. And isn't it nice that someone else out there believes?" Then I got to thinking about all the people that ask me how you're doing. They ask how I'm doing. They tell me they're praying for me. They tell me stories of their own struggles. They give me hope. They help me believe that all this good recovery will last.

So, while it's true that we do not get casseroles or prayer shawls as we might if we were experiencing some other illness, we do get many words of comfort. Most people really do let me know they're in this with us. And that they're rooting for us.

I so appreciate them. We are not alone.

Love,
Mom

Day 120

Dear David,

Again, I am a little late in writing. I was going to write you a New Year's letter, on New Year's Eve, of course.

Plans and people got in the way.

Anyway, I went to church on New Year's Eve. I prayed like the sinner that I am. Said a ferocious farewell to 2014 and all the pain it carried. Prayed a hopeful hello to 2015. Geez, God, could we just make this year a little better than the last?

Then I thought, "Well, poor old 2014. It wasn't all bad. Pretty darn bad, but not a complete write-off."

Every night I go to bed with my list of anxieties swirling around in my head. I've had some success turning this mental spigot off by writing in a gratitude journal. Each night I scribble down the good stuff, and most nights I fill the page. (OK, so the book is very, very small, but I do fill it!)

So, here, in appreciation of 2014, were the good things:

- You found the Mission.

- You have been sober for ninety days!
- Dad and I have each found good support groups.
- We have found endless support from others, especially people at church.
- Auntie and Ellen bought a house near ours. We love spending time with them.
- You are so much fun to have around these days!
- Patch, our cat (whom we now call "the last animal standing"), is healthy and happy and here!
- You and your sister love each other again.
- We are all healthy, happy, and together.

Now, that wasn't so hard, was it?

So I'll say good-bye to 2014, and thank the year for all it has given us. But the good-bye is certainly said with a sigh of relief.

Let's keep this good stuff going for 2015, shan't we?

Love,
Mom

Day 122

Dear David,

Last night we invited the Steins to our house for dinner and games. This is our new way of getting together with friends on a Saturday night.

It used to be that the four of us would meet at a restaurant for dinner. But this became sort of problematic for a couple of reasons. First, the restaurants we go to are invariably noisy. It is very tiresome to yell, "Yes, thank goodness he is no longer living on the streets!" or "We don't know when it all started, we just know…" Anyway, you get the idea. It is very stressful, not to mention it turns more than a few unwanted heads our way.

Then there is the silence that follows. After one more bit of bad news, everyone at the table suddenly becomes very interested in what's on their plates, and we all start eating with gusto, as if our Caesar salads are the best ones to come along in a very long time.

So, now we have taken to inviting people to our house for take-out Chinese and a rousing game of Hearts. We are not ashamed of talking about you; we are just kind of tired of talking about you. This night of games gets us out of discussion mode and into some forced fun.

And it has been fun! So I suppose I should thank you for that.

Love,
Mom

Day 124

Dear David,

Have you ever had one of those dreams that is so realistic, the feelings it causes stay with you all day long? Last night I had a dream like that. And I have been in a cranky mood all day.

Here's the dream, or maybe I should call it a nightmare. You were doing all the good things you were supposed to be doing to lead a clean and sober life. You were going to meetings, hanging out with sober friends, getting a job.

Only, in the dream, it turned out it was all just a lie. You were using. You were living with Joe again. The job search? All a sham. In fact, the whole new sober life was a ruse.

And here is why the nightmare has had me in a bad mood all day: it felt so real. Because, in fact, we have been down this road before. Just when we thought everything was going OK, the rug gets pulled out from under us. So we remain ever vigilant.

I'm not saying that I don't believe all the good things you're doing and all the great things we're experiencing are real. I'm saying that, still, the mistrust lies *just* below the surface. Like a shark waiting to rear its ugly head above the ocean's calm surface.

There's nothing we can do about it, except tell ourselves that, just for today, the good stuff is real. And if it's not real, well, we'll survive the attack. We have before, and we will again.

Love,
Mom

Day 125

Dear David,

Well, that was quite a night, wasn't it? Celebrating ninety days of sobriety. And we celebrated where you began your recovery: at the Mission.

The evening started out with the usual crazy sing-along: "Amazing Grace," "I'll Fly Away," and "Will the Circle Be Unbroken?," along with all the others. I'm always up for a sing-along, but usually within a more sedate, Lutheran-like atmosphere. And Dad is *never* up for a sing-along. But I smiled last night... Dad was singing as loud as I was. And this time we didn't spend our time self-consciously glancing around with our mouths hanging open at this motley group of recovering addicts.

I gave a big hug to Mike G., my forever friend who first got you to the Mission. A hug also went to your old roommate Kevin, four months sober, who played games and ate turkey with us at Thanksgiving. There was Andrew, six months sober, who just couldn't stop smiling, and shaking our hands and hugging us, exclaiming how good it was to have "Dave" back. Jess (eighteen months sober), your sponsor, took my hand in his. What a smile. Mike L. was happy to see you. Michael C. equally happy. Rob (celebrating one year) gave me a big, loud greeting. I was delighted when Bonnie, she of "I wish I had rock tumbler," gave me an affectionate embrace. There were so many smiles and pats on the back; even you professed to be a little embarrassed by the "celebrity" attention of it.

So, for ninety days you have been clean and sober. And for ninety days you have felt the love of God, and the love of so many people, especially your brothers at the Mission.

And, I am proud to say, Dad and I have ninety days to celebrate too. We celebrate the love of God, the love of the brothers at the Mission, and the love of friends and family. We celebrate that we can go to the Mission and feel comfortable with those we never would have before. We can see someone on the corner asking for a handout, and give him or her money, because we know our son was once that person, and we want that person's life to be saved, or to be at least that much more comfortable. We truly understand, "one day at a time."

We celebrate that just for today, we are a family again. And we have our David back. Praise God.

Love you,
Mom

Dear David,

Last night, at my line-dance class, a woman named Roz said, "I'm praying for your son." I said, "Well, thank you. He just got his ninety-day medallion!" She said, "Yes, Julia told me. She keeps up with you on Facebook." This was so remarkable to me. First, that two people I barely know, but dance with every week, talk about me. And they talk about you. And, even more, they pray for you. I mean, they don't even know you!

The graciousness of total strangers is astounding to me. I am so deeply and profoundly touched.

After class, I showed Roz a picture of you at the Mission. I said, "Here is my David." I wanted her to know your name (did she already know it?); I wanted her to picture your beautiful smile as she prayed for you.

I think she was happy to see it, but it didn't seem to matter all that much. Because I think that she knew of someone in need, the son of this unfamiliar woman who dances in the row behind her every week, and she decided to pray. That is pure kindness. And pure belief.

I pray every day for the belief Roz must have that her prayers for you will make a difference, as they clearly have. And I pray for the grace to pray for other strangers who, like you and me, need all the prayers they can get.

Love,
Mom

Day 128

Dear David,

On Monday night, Dad and I attended our monthly "I Am the Parent of an Addicted Child" meeting. As you know, these really have been enormously helpful. There is nothing like the sigh of relief you experience as you hear that other parents are going through, or have gone through, the same hell you have.

Anyway, the leader was telling her story, a long and very depressing descent into drugs, while she was a young model living in New York City, of all things. We get to the uplifting part—you know, she finds sobriety, lives the clean life—and then, as happens in EVERY ONE of these stories, comes the fall. She gets BORED. After two and a half years of living sober, she gets bored. Falls off the wagon. Big time. Runs off with a drug dealer, all sorts of things.

This is what they call RELAPSE. When you were in treatment, and Dad and I were going through the parent program, we were often warned of the big ugly monster named Relapse. It was always discussed as a foregone conclusion: "When your child relapses...," never "If your child relapses..." Are you kidding? We're going through all this crap just to know we're gonna have to do it again? It's like recovering from open-heart surgery, only to know they're going to rip you open again in six months.

So, here was this leader who had it all, and I'm sure her parents were saying, "Whew, we got through that... and with no relapses!" I mean, who wouldn't say that after two and a half years? Can we never relax? Dad summed it up perfectly when he said, "I just wish David would hurry up and relapse now so we can get it over with." That makes sense; just get it done while the wound is fresh.

Of course, I don't mean that. At least, mostly I don't mean that.

But honestly, could we skip the relapse part? Or if not, could you just get it over with now? Make it really fast and painless?

Just a suggestion.

Love,
Mom

Day 129

Dear David,

Today we went to see your psychiatrist, Dr. B. When she asked you how your job at the coffee shop was going, you said, "Fine, but I only make $9.50 an hour. I made a lot more money when I was dealing drugs."

Really? Is this a comparison you really want to make? Like some wistful look back at the good ol' days?

Dr. B. let it go without comment. I did too, although I was surely stunned into silence.

Love,
Mom

Dear David,

Last night at my line-dance class, I talked to Harris, an African American man who is proud to say that he has been sober for five years, following many years of addiction. I told him your story, and how you got sober. I told him that treatment at the Center just didn't work for you, and that it was the good men at the Mission and the promise of God that saved your life. I told him that you didn't like the Center one bit.

Harris said, "It's all just political," referring to the Center. I said, "Well, to me it was all just financial." He replied, "Same thing."

Places like the Center work for a lot of people. But for the likes of you, it was a machine. The longer you stayed, the more money they made. The Mission was simple. "Stay until you get better." And it worked. No politics, no money. Just simple recovery, with the help of good fellowship and the promises of God.

To that, Harris would undoubtedly say, "Amen."

Love,
Mom

Day 131

Dear David,

Last night you called me. Actually, you called our home phone. Dad answered. "Hey, Bud!" he enthused, at which point you asked to talk to Mom.

This was a red flag. One that should have sent me running in the other direction.

It always means one thing: you need to vent, and for some reason Mom is the best place to do that.

You start right in, no niceties here like, "Hi, Mom, how are you?" No, it's a rant from the get-go. About how much you hate where you're living, how much you hate the guys, how much you hate the counselor. I do as I have been instructed. I mirror: "Sounds like you are really frustrated," I reframe: "Perhaps for today this roommate is doing some annoying things," I sympathize: "This sounds pretty tough." But that only makes the bull see red.

More spewing, until the final act: you hang up on me. Just like that.

Gee, here I was enjoying reading the newspaper, sitting in front of the fire, cat in my lap. And minutes later, I have been gored by the raging bull.

You would think I'd learn. The next time I see that red bull running toward me, I better get out of the way.

Love,
Mom

Day 133

Dear David,

OK, so here is the latest accusation you have lobbed my way. I nag. In fact, I am a nag. Nag? When I think of "nag," I think of a lady in a housecoat nagging her husband and children to hang up their coats, to wipe up the bathroom floor, to walk the dog. Over and over again, this lady nags. Nag, nag, nag.

And here's the real rub: Dad agrees with you! When I tell him with indignation that you are accusing me of nagging, he agrees.

So, after much "discussion," I've learned what nagging means to you. I ask you if you've done something, like, "Have you brushed your teeth?" This after you have rolled out of bed, hair all askew, still in your sweatpants from the night before. You have overslept and need to meet with someone. Well, it is only natural for a person to wonder if you have brushed away that offensive morning breath. How about this: "Have you unpacked the clothes you brought home from the Mission?" This after the bin holding them has sat there for a week in the middle of your bedroom.

151

I could go on and on with examples, as indeed you could, but I will not. I refuse to explain myself except to say, *someone* has to remind you to do these things. And if nagging means that I tell you or ask you to do things, then just write me down as a nag. And just because you lived on the streets, at the Mission, and now a sober house, does not mean I have turned in my license to nag when you come home to visit.

So, here is what I've said to Dad, and what I'll say to you. I am the mom. As the mom, I get to ask if you have eaten lunch, if you have buttoned your coat, and if you have made your bed. (Because, in all probability, you have done none of these things). Take it or leave it. I am what I am.

As I told Dad, you two are free to roll your eyes and gossip about me behind my back. But you are not free to call me a nag, which by the way rhymes with hag.

Love,
Mom

Day 134

Dear David,

I have not talked to you in two days, read it, *two days!* This is a good thing, right?

I mean, we are working toward independence (on your part) and detachment (on my part), and what better way to do that than to *stop talking* (or texting) each other every day?

The problem is, I'm a little wary of this silence. The last time we cut off communication, you were God knows where.

But honestly, it has only been forty-eight hours. What a crazed woman I have become.

So, enjoy your time away from the apron strings. And I will enjoy the freedom too.

But do call me when you get the chance. Just to let me know you're fine.

Love you,
Mom

Day 135

Dear David,

I had the strangest day yesterday. I was *bored*. All day long.

I wondered, why was my day so uneventful, so lacking in purpose? And I think I have it figured out: I didn't have you to worry about. I didn't have to call you, a therapist, a doctor, a treatment center, a pharmacy. I didn't have to call the director of the sober house, the person who handles your money, the person in charge of helping you get a job. Because in this new attitude of detachment, I'm letting someone else, namely you, as well as all the good people around you, make those decisions! I'm letting you and your team take the reins!

I am free! I am detached! I am bored.

I complained to Dad last night before dinner about feeling bored. He nodded, and then proceeded to say grace.

He prayed, "Thank you, God, for the opportunity to feel bored. Not everyone has the luxury to feel boredom in their lives, and for that we are truly thankful."

Touché.

So, I am off to apply for a job. Or to take up knitting.

Thank you, David, for letting me be bored by taking care of your own life.

Love,
Mom

Dear David,

I heard the greatest saying yesterday: "If you don't want to get stung, don't put your nose in the beehive."

Boy, oh boy, doesn't that just apply to me? Wouldn't you agree that most of my problems have been because I have stuck my nose in your beehive?

I know you would agree.

Here's to a new year for us... one without any bee stings at all.

Love you,
Mom

Day 138

Dear David,

Yesterday I saw a big advertisement on the side of a bus. It encouraged me to go to Ely for a winter vacation. And it made me intensely sad. Because you were all set to go to college in Ely. It was such a perfect fit. Because you love the outdoors, and you love winter, and you love being just that much "outside the box"... living in a small town on the edge of civilization. You are supposed to be there now.

And then, darn, all this addiction stuff got in the way. And I swear I really am happy you live in a sober house in town. But, I am really sad to give up that dream of my boy in Ely.

I told Dad about this. He said, "Well, it might still happen." And he's right of course. You may still live the dream I had for you in Ely.

I guess when they say, "Just for today," they know what they're talking about. Just for today you are sober, happy, living in a supportive community, and you have a job.

My dream for you is deferred. Or changed. Or just not in the cards. Or maybe it will still happen.

Guess we'll leave all that to God. In the meantime, I am living one day at a time.

Love,
Mom

Dear David,

Last night I had dinner at church, as I do every Wednesday night.

I sat at a table with a woman whose son is your age. He is going to the University of Iowa. Her other son, two years older, is going to St. Olaf. They are both so happy.

She asked about you. I told her about how you've been sober four months; how you have been living in a sober house.

She knew your story. She looked into my eyes and said, "I'm so glad." I thanked her, because I could tell she meant it. And it was so kind of her to say that.

But I wish I could have told her about your carefree days at college.

Love you,
Mom

Day 141

Dear David,

As so often happens since you've started recovery, I was providing limo service for you and one of your "brothers." This means I am driving, you are sitting in the front passenger seat, and the invariably cheerful passenger is sitting in the back.

This week's sunny topic: homelessness. This guy, Hunter, said, "Yah, before I got here, I had been living on the streets of Seattle for a year... I actually really liked it." Well, I just couldn't let that one go. "You *enjoyed* living on the streets?", I asked, to which he responded, "Oh yah, it was pretty fun."

I have two words for Hunter, or is it one? *Bullshit.* He is either a) a big fat liar, b) delusional, or c) still using drugs. If nothing else, he has certainly not spent a winter living homeless in Minnesota.

Then, of course, you had to put in your two cents. About how notoriously awful it is to live on the streets of St. Paul. How the cops around here are known for being especially hostile to homeless people. You started in with your story, how you were constantly harassed by cops when you were trying to sleep in bus shelters. Where else were you supposed to go, you wondered. Let's just file that under "TMI": *too much information.* I do not need to know about the places you slept when you were not at home.

So, Hunter, shut up. Or at least talk about more cheery topics like world hunger, war, or crime. You're not fooling me. Homelessness is not fun.

Love,
Mom

Dear David,

This morning I had another experience with "TMI." I was at the copy shop making photocopies of your drug/ alcohol assessment, which needs to be sent to the district court in Waterloo, Iowa... part of the requirements to settle last summer's DWI.

I had made a promise to myself that I would *not* read this multipage report. Why rehash old times, open old wounds?

Even so, out of the photocopier came page after page of your using life, just begging to be read. I couldn't help it; I peeked over to see the dirty details. TMI. I did stop looking when the stories just got too painful to imagine.

Like a hot potato, I plucked up those pieces of incriminating evidence, stapled them together, and stuffed them into the large envelope, ready to be mailed off. Good riddance.

I'm glad those days are over. I'm not ashamed of the things you did; I'm just saddened. And I'm even happier that those days are behind you. May it ever be so.

Love,
Mom

Day 145

Dear David,

Who knew that a walk outside could be so wonderful? Dad and I are still smiling (both inside and outside) thinking about this miraculous trek through the Minnesota woods.

On Sunday, I suggested to Dad that we take a hike *outside*. As you know, I am not a fan of cold weather; the slightest gust of wind sends me back into the recliner with a cup of coffee and a book. But the sun was shining, finally, and the temperature was almost above freezing, so I decided to throw caution to that cold wind.

I invited you to come along, and you said yes!

I was thoroughly bundled up; you laughed and assured me I would be "way too hot." I advised you that you "really should wear a hat," to which you replied with a good-natured roll of the eyes and a "Yes, Mom."

Here's the thing that's making me smile: we had such a naturally good time! No forced conversation, no recriminations, no dread. I will admit that the nasty shadow of "When will the other shoe drop?"

occasionally reared its ugly head, but it really was so far in the background, I almost forgot it.

The air was chilly, the sun was shining, the snow crunched beneath our feet. We stopped to look at the beaver-gnawed trees and the young bald eagle soaring far above us.

We talked, we laughed. Gee, what a blessing that day was.

I texted you later, telling you what a good time we had. You said you felt the same. Then you said, "I love you."

Well, that's all a mom needs, really.

See you next weekend.

Love,
Mom

Day 147

Dear David,

People often ask me how you're doing, to which I answer, "Just great!," because it's true. But, oh, I do wish they wouldn't push further. Because beyond "great," "OK," "fine," or "struggling," I have no other responses to give.

Here is a list of questions for which I have no answers:

- What are his plans for the future?
- Do you think he'll stay sober?
- Will he go back to school?
- How long will he live in sober housing?
- Do you think he'll get a different job?
- Will he start driving again?
- How about dating?

These are all very well-intentioned questions, and I do appreciate them. But if there is one thing this disease of addiction has taught me, it's that there's a whole lot of mystery in our lives.

As someone who likes *control,* who likes to know what's happening, why it's happening, and surely wants to know what will be happening in the future, this is difficult. Nearly impossible. But your journey, our journey, has taught me to live with the mystery. This "just for today" stuff is what it's all about.

I trust you are doing fine today. And I pray with all my heart that you'll be fine tomorrow. And truly I am counting on the fact that in the end, you'll have the life you were meant to have, which is a good one.

But I don't know. The truth is, we *all* really don't know what will happen in the future. Beyond "great" today, there is just a whole lot of "I don't know."

I'm learning to live with it.

Love,

Mom

Day 148

Dear David,

Every week, Matt, the counselor from your sober house, calls me to give me an update.

Here's the deal: the stuff Matt tells me gets stuck in my craw, and I can't shake it. Like, "David seems to be having trouble making connections with the guys in the house," or "David is not doing enough to find a job." I do think he tries to sprinkle in some *positive* comments, but by the time the concerns have aired, my head is buzzing so loud, I can't hear that good stuff.

My immediate response is "I MUST FIX THIS." Plain and simple. I must call you and counsel you on how to make friends. I must call the guy in the house that is supposed to be helping you find a job. I must come over and tuck you in at night.

Then my other job is to obsess about it all day.

As you can see, I've got "some work" to do with my therapist.

But Dad came up with a great idea. It came to him as I met him at the door, week after week, all frazzled and worried and convinced you were doomed. He said,

"Why don't you have Matt call me?" Brilliant. So now Matt calls Dad. And every week Dad tells me you are doing fine, because, in fact, you really are.

Love,
Mom

Day 150

Dear David,

Today is the Super Bowl. You, of course, do not care. Actually, the whole family does not much care, because we do not much like football.

But what we do care about is the party at K.'s house, to which we have been invited since you were a boy. This year we were not invited. Now, there may be all sorts of reasons why this happened, like maybe they didn't even have it, but it stings, it really does. Because this lack of invitation comes at the end of a year in which I have felt neglected by K., and that neglect started with your drug use.

K. was a second mother to you. And I do not use that phrase lightly. You and her son were best friends. They live down the block, and you were just as likely to be at K.'s house as your own when you were a child. K. listened to you, taught you manners that I was not able to instill, gave you advice. She loved you. And now she ignores you. Or it seems that way to me. I mean, how hard would it be for her to call me or you and ask how you're doing?

A few months ago, K. and I had a conversation; we crossed paths as we were walking our dogs. We talked about everything but you. She never asked.

Dad says that some people just cannot stand to be around bad news. And your news surely was pretty bad for a while.

You tell me you still talk to her on the phone once in a while. You called her from the Mission. You've talked to her son, your ex-best friend. And you are not angry about this, this seemingly neglectful relationship. I think you should be, but then again, your path to acceptance seems a lot less treacherous than mine. Certainly less painful.

When I told my friend John about this, he nodded his head in recognition. His son Kyle got into big trouble with drugs. Suddenly, their circle of friends shrunk... considerably. No one wants to hear the bad news, darn it.

Well, you are certainly good news to me.

Love you,
Mom

Dear David,

Remember how I wrote about the kid who had gone to recover in California? I laughed because I could not imagine an easier place to recover than California. Who needs to drink when you can lie on the beach and soak up sun?

When I told you about that, you replied, "Actually, it would be really hard to recover in such a warm and beautiful place. When I'm on a beach or poolside or anywhere warm or sunny, it makes me want to get high." Hmmm.

I do get your point. There is nothing nicer than a margarita while lounging on a sandy beach.

I stand corrected. Recovery is difficult no matter where you do it.

Love,
Mom

Day 153

Dear David,

Today I'm mad at Dad. I was mad at him yesterday, and the day before. I just cannot get rid of this resentment... it needs to be talked out, I know.

So, what does this have to do with you? Well, everything, of course, and perhaps nothing. Because before your addiction became apparent in this family, Dad and I really didn't fight that much. And if we did, we resolved things pretty quickly. But now with this family disease infecting each of us in its particular way, these arguments pop up, and are slow to settle down.

On Sunday, while you were visiting us at our house, you were in a bad mood. You said, "I don't know what's bothering me, but I need to leave now." I understood the code: you were upset about something and needed to be out of the family circle for a while. I don't like it when you leave, but I've come to accept it. It doesn't happen often, and it's kind of painful, but it's a strategy that works. You and I know it's a whole lot better than having you hang around, fuming and moping.

Anyway, a few hours after you left, Dad informed me that you'd left because of what I'd said. I was stunned. Then I was angry. I've looked at this from every angle, and yet I cannot see how the things I said (what were they, actually?) caused you to hightail it out of here.

But then, that's not the point, is it? The point is, Dad was upset. He needed someone to blame. He is afraid of getting mad at you, for fear you will leave on a more permanent basis. So, it comes to me. And then I get mad at him and mad at you. Christine gets mad because once again you have disrupted the family... well, you get it. It is indeed a family disease, and this disease has us either walking on eggshells or lobbing blame at one another. Even after you have been sober for over one hundred days!

So, who is to blame but ourselves? You were smart to get out of here. And we were left with the ripples that action caused. We did not handle it well.

I know, it's a family disease. We all play a part, and we all need to be part of the solution.

But I am still mad at Dad.

Love,
Mom

Day 155

Dear David,

Yesterday, the strangest thing happened, don't you think? We went to see Dr. B., your psychiatrist. We were talking about your meds, and your addiction, and your recovery. Then Dr. B. got all teary. It turns out that her son's best friend from high school overdosed on drugs the night before!

We were stunned. Geez, does this addiction stuff happen everywhere and to everyone? Even the best friend of your psychiatrist's son? I know there are a few degrees of separation here, but still.

So then Dr. B. said, "Don't go back to the drugs. It's just not frickin' worth it." Again, we were stunned. This major head of the psychiatry department, the one that gets quoted all the time in the newspaper, the one who is always on the top of the list of best psychiatrists says, "It's just not frickin' worth it"?

Well, I guess there's just no better way to say it, is there?

Pay attention, boy.

Love,
Mom

Dear David,

Right now you are upstairs in your boyhood (just when did it become *boyhood*?) bed. You are sick. You called me yesterday to tell me you weren't feeling well, and "If it wouldn't be too much trouble, could you take me to the doctor?" I thought, "Are you kidding? Finally, something *concrete* I can do to lessen this kid's suffering!"

I took you to the doctor; he wrote a prescription; and I brought you home to bed.

Last night, as Dad and I were turning out the light he said, "I'm glad to have David here." And I had to agree. I was happy to have you here so that I could take care of you in some way; getting you a drink, a pillow, or a blanket. And Dad was happy to have you here just because it's nice to have you here. It is.

Get well soon.

Love,
Mom

Day 159

Dear David,

On Monday, Dad and I have been invited to share our story (which naturally revolves around you) at the "I Am the Parent of an Addicted Child" meeting.

Now, this is another one of those experiences I never expected to have—telling our surprising story of addiction and recovery in front of a bunch of families who are, in fact, surprised to be sitting there themselves.

Anyway, it's one more to add to my list of things I never ever thought I would experience, which now includes a homeless child, court, jail, near death by car accident, total destruction of aforementioned car, arrests, police reports, treatment, plea deals, sober houses, probation, urine tests, emergency rooms, sober high school, court appointed attorney, the Treatment Center, the Union Gospel Mission, and speaking to other parents of addicts.

As I said, it's all just a little surprising.

Love you,
Mom

Day 160

Dear David,

Yesterday you told me that warm weather is a trigger for you.

This term *trigger* is relatively new to me. It indicates something that makes you want to get high. The metaphor must have something to do with pulling a trigger on a gun at the start of a race: "On your marks, get set, go!" Or maybe it's a gun that you hold to your head.

In any case, it's that thing that makes you want to go back down User Lane. I wonder, what is it about the promise of a warm spring that makes you want to enter an altered state of consciousness?

And here I was looking forward to spring. Now I have to dread it, darn it.

Love,
Mom

Day 163

Dear David,

Yesterday I got an e-mail from the mom of a one of your fellow "inmates" at the Center. Andrea and I had been in the family program together. She has since returned to Rhode Island, while her son, Paul, is doing more treatment in California.

I asked her how Paul was doing. She said, "Fine, but sometimes I think he is just waiting us out. Like, he goes through the motions, does the treatment, does the program, and then when no one is looking, he will just go right back to his old ways." She admitted, "I'm just waiting for the other shoe to drop."

I know what she means. You really are doing so great, but there is not a parent in recovery that's not looking over his or her shoulder, waiting for the next tsunami to hit.

We pray for the best, but sadly, are prepared for the worst.

Love,
Mom

Day 165

Dear David,

Here's what most people do not understand about addiction: it has nothing to do with how nice a person is. Or how well behaved. Or their accomplishments.

A few years ago, when Dad first told our next-door-neighbor, Mr. M., about you being in treatment for drug addiction, he was so surprised; well, I guess, come to think of it, we all were. But he came back to Dad the next week and said, "I just can't stop thinking about David. He is such a great kid! How could he be abusing drugs? It just doesn't make sense." A few months later, Dad was visiting an old friend, Melissa, and her husband. After catching them up on recent events, their response was the same: "Such a nice kid. How could this have happened?" These responses are typical of what we hear daily.

Yes, addiction hits even the nicest of us, the Eagle Scouts and the valedictorians. No use wondering how it could have hit such a nice boy, and such a nice family.

We just have to deal with it. And we do.

Love,
Mom

Day 168

Dear David,

You may know that at church we have a prayer list. Every Sunday, the yellow insert inside the program lists the names of people who have requested prayers during the week. I added your name a number of months ago. It says, "David H., in recovery." So I presume every week these faithful members are indeed praying for my son.

Here's my quandary: when do I take you off the list? You have been sober for five months. Is that long enough? When will I know it's safe to remove your name? Will taking you off the list jinx your recovery? And will continued prayers ensure that your sobriety will last?

I don't want to be superstitious, but there you have it; I am. Because it sometimes all feels so precarious, this business of recovery. One wrong move to upset the apple cart and we're right back into relapse.

I have no answers. Only questions.

I guess I'll just keep you on the list for now.

Love,
Mom

Day 171

Dear David,

Here's another thing I know about addiction: it has nothing to do with how good or bad your parents were. At least that's what I keep telling myself.

Last night, Dad and I were at the monthly "I Am the Parent of an Addicted Child" meeting. There was some anxious discussion amongst the parents along the lines of "Where did we go wrong? What could we have done differently?" One dad spoke up, saying, "I am a recovering alcoholic. Let me tell you once and for all you had *nothing* to do with your child's addiction. I would have become a drunk no matter what." This, of course, elicited a collective sigh of relief.

Addiction really does strike randomly. It can hit the ones with great parents, rotten parents, and anyone in between.

You know we did our best.

Love you,
Mom

Day 174

Dear David,

Yesterday we had a new participant in our Al-Anon group. His name was Steve, and his son, Jacob, was coming home, having just completed treatment for drug addiction.

I talked to Steve after the meeting. I told him that you are Jacob's age and had been in the same program, at the same treatment center, this past summer. I wondered how he was feeling about Jacob coming home. "Great!" he said. "I've missed him like crazy!" No hint of fear or trepidation. I admit I wanted to offer comfort; the thought of having my recovered son reenter my house makes me shudder. Don't get me wrong; I missed you like crazy too. I just did not miss all the lies, missing objects, and havoc that resulted from us living together.

Am I being too cynical? Is Steve being too naïve? Well, it is not for me to judge, is it, although I surely will.

For us, you coming home meant entering your old environment, filled with old triggers, old "friends," old feelings, and your old crazy family. It was too much for all of us, which is why you are happily ensconced in a sober house. We all like it that way.

I wish Steve and Jacob and their whole family the best. It will take a lot of work. But again, who am I to judge?

Love,
Mom

Day 177

Dear David,

Today's troubling news headline: "Meth Was Downfall of Manhunt Gunman..."

The story in the newspaper is about a former meth addict, named David, who had been clean for seven years. He had worked steadily for the past four years at the local auto-towing shop, eventually becoming "tow lead."

The shop's owner said, "He was a great success story, a second-chance story of how he kicked meth in the gut."

But then, a year ago, David started using meth again. When he was seen in a car with a handgun on the front seat, someone called 911. Officers responded, resulting in a shootout with David. He shot himself.

I'll bet David's parents had been thinking, "Whew, we finally got through that! Look... he has been sober seven years, has a good job, and is a nice guy. We can finally cross that worry off our list."

Turns out we can never cross this worry of relapse off our list.

As the poetic shop owner said, "At the end, he lost hope. But if you ever got to meet him, he was just nice; he had a servant's heart. But the demon took him over."

Just a reminder, and a painful one at that; this addiction lasts a lifetime.

Love,
Mom

Day 180

Dear David,

Yesterday, my friend Dan (the Story Man) gave me the opportunity to write for his blog about a transformation in my life. Of course, I jumped at the chance to write and, of course, that transformation had to do with you.

Here's how the piece starts: "There was a time, not too long ago, when I thought, 'This is it. I am falling apart. I am going to break up into a million little pieces, and blow away.'" Of course, that is how I felt when you left the Center and were living God-knows-where.

You know, back in those days I honestly did have the physical sensation that I was made of glass, and that I was going to break into a million little pieces.

But that was 180 days ago. Since then you have found recovery, and with the help of my family, supportive friends, Al-Anon, our church, the "I am a Parent of an Addicted Child" meetings, lots of prayer, and all these letters that I have written to you, so have I. Not complete recovery, mind you, but recovery one day at a time.

I do feel whole again. I feel kicked and beaten at times, but I know I will no longer shatter.

Your life is yours, and my life is mine.
I love you very much.

Love,
Mom

"Unbreakable Glass: A Mother's Story"

There was a time, not too long ago, when I thought, "This is it. I am falling apart. I am going to break up into a million little pieces, and blow away."

Months earlier, my husband and I had issued an ultimatum to our eighteen-year-old son, David: go to treatment, or leave. He left. I thought, "Well, we'll just wait him out. And when he finally decides to enter treatment, life will be good." My happiness rested on David getting the help he needed.

After a week of David living on the street, I was overjoyed that our patience had won out; he entered outpatient treatment for drug abuse. Finally, some peace and joy at our house. Only someone forgot to give David the script. Because after three days, he walked out.

I was pretty upset. Still, I thought, "Just get him into treatment, and everything will be OK." We waited him out for another three weeks; he got hungry and cold, and decided to enter inpatient treatment. Life could get back to good again.

Except that after seven weeks of inpatient treatment, David walked away. He called me and calmly told me was leaving treatment. And he did.

So began the most excruciating period of my life as a mother. For three weeks, I had no idea where he was. If he was dead or alive. That's when I felt as if I were made of glass. One more piece of bad news, and they would be sweeping me off the floor.

So, since there was nothing I could do, I started a blog. I wrote letters to David describing my sadness, my anger, my bewilderment. I asked him, "Really, wouldn't it just be easier to go into treatment than to live like a hobo?" Those letters helped me chronicle a life that I could not believe I was living. Arrest? Jail time? Near fatal car accidents? Not my kid. Not my life.

David never wrote back, largely because I kept the letters online, but even so, he surely would not have wanted to correspond.

But other parents wrote back. They told me their painfully similar stories. Some of their stories had happy endings. Others did not.

Reading their stories helped me to see that I was not alone. And, even more, they taught me that all of us as parents, no matter how fine our powers of persuasion, were completely powerless to change these kids.

These parents had survived, no matter the outcome with their children. They were hurting, but they were not broken.

Over time, David did decide to get better. He chose recovery. On his own. He has been sober for over one hundred days.

And here's the strange thing: by the time he made this decision, I had figured out that my happiness did not depend on it. I mean, it's awfully nice to have him here among the living, and I do mean that quite literally. But, and don't tell him I said this, if he starts using again, I will feel very sad. But I will not shatter. I may have to keep writing about it, but I will not break.

He found his own sobriety. He can find it again. And my happiness does not have to depend on it.

First published in Daniel Maurer's blog *Transformation is Real*, www.transformation-is-real.com.

About the Author

Martha Wegner lives and writes in St. Paul, Minnesota. She is the author of numerous articles and books, including the upcoming essay collection, *A Word in Edgewise: Life in between Raising Kids, Keeping a Home, and Staying Sane* (Beaver's Pond Press). For more information, visit her website at www.marthawegner.com.